Walk for Life

WALK FOR LIFE

The Lifetime Walking Program for a Healthy Body and Mind

Deena and David Balboa

Illustrated by Linda Knox

A Perigee Book

Not all exercises are suitable for everyone, and this or any other exercise program may result in injury. To reduce the risk of injury in your case, consult your doctor before beginning the exercise program, especially if you have any serious medical condition or if you are taking medication. Responsibility for any adverse affects or unforeseen consequences resulting from the use of any information contained herein is expressly disclaimed.

Perigee Books
are published by
The Putnam Publishing Group
200 Madison Avenue
New York, NY 10016

Walking logo by Anthony Kosner
Book design by Sheree Goodman

Library of Congress Cataloging-in-Publication-Data

Balboa, Deena.
Walk for life: the lifetime walking program for a healthy body and mind/ by Deena and David Balboa.
p.   cm.
Includes bibliographical references.
ISBN 0-399-51622-0
1. Walking—Health aspects 2. Physical fitness. I. Balboa, David. II. Title.
RA781.65.B35   1990   90-6880 CIP
613.7′ 176—dc20

Printed in the United States of America
1   2   3   4   5   6   7   8   9   10

This book is printed on acid-free paper.
∞

ACKNOWLEDGMENTS

To Tracey M. McCullough, whose brilliance and expertise in the field of walking lit the way for us as we stepped out with our innovative ideas.

To Gary Westerfield for generously sharing his vast knowledge about the sport of race walking.

To Kon Berner, Linda Braun, Tom Gustafson, Karen Luxton, Oren Klaber, Anthony Kosner, Robin Ladas, Aliza Schwadron for the many hours of help and dedication they contributed.

To our agent, Bob Silverstein, for his generous support and guidance throughout the project.

To our copyeditor, Claire Winecoff, for her meticulous and thorough detail to the manuscript.

To our editor, Adrienne Ingrum, for her insight in welcoming into the publishing field two expert walkers who were fledgling writers, many sincere thanks for her patience with our work.

DEDICATION

TO
Dominick Bosco
for his spirit,
for his creativity,
for his friendship.

CONTENTS

PREFACE

In late spring of 1986, I received a message that a couple had arrived at Rodale looking for *Prevention* editor in chief, Mark Bricklin, to discuss the newly formed Prevention Walking Club. There were murmurings of "psychotherapists" and "walking style." As the newly appointed editor for the club, anxious to unearth any possible editorial angle (In the beginning I was always terrified of running out of material. Little did I know that walking would be a major research theme for years to come.) I ran (rather I walked rapidly) downtown to catch them eating in a little vegetarian restaurant.

At that time they were David Balboa and Deena Karabell, two New York City psychotherapists out on a limb in eastern Pennsylvania—exploring the possibility of expounding on their very personal perceptions about walking with Rodale Press. They spoke about style, technique, and the ability of the body to speak for the mind and emotions. And how proper posture and improved style could feed back to both the person and the world—creating an improved sense of self. They'd experienced it—worked with it, knew it. They were just waiting for the scientific world of test and measures to catch up with them.

David was still formulating his way of talking about this style. Somehow, in the course of the conversation, "Sambawalking" was born and I knew I had an intriguing article to write. I took a photographer into New York City and met David and Deena in Central Park where they coached a group of walkers in the rhythmic and dance-like style (later to become the Balboa walking approach). I tried to walk with the group, but they seemed to sail effortlessly out of my reach. I was huffing and puffing and they were gliding along. They stopped and took turns analyzing style and gait as David astutely pointed out ways to improve their walk.

"Sambawalking in Central Park" was printed in the *Prevention Magazine* Walking Club annual, *Walker's World*, in the spring of 1987, and David and Deena joined walking history. Coverage continued—both in Rodale Press publications and in other media around the country.

A year later, David and Deena were married and I began to work with them personally. The first time David analyzed my walking style, he mimicked my duck-footed style. Later he helped me loosen my hips and relax my shoulders. I observed my gait and carriage change over the course of a year from slouched and awkward to tall and sure-footed, relaxed and graceful. For the first time in my life someone actually complimented me on my posture. Internal changes were occurring too, both in response to walking well and as I worked with Deena and experienced her astounding insights and healing capabilities.

The insights put forth in this book may seem astonishingly simple. As usual the proof is in the pudding. When editor Bob Rodale had a session with David, he scoffed internally at the idea of being "taught" to walk. While on a trip to Russia, he experimented with the walking approach and, as he put it, "felt better!" and began to rethink his resistance to learning to walk "well." I've seen numerous people experience the power of walking well with David and Deena's help and I am immensely pleased that this book will make their insight available to anyone with the time and interest to read about it.

When the walking phenomenon began to snowball, critics scoffed at the idea of teaching people to improve such a rudimentary act. I particularly remember the comment suggesting that soon we'd have "breathing clubs" (I thought it was funny too, except I found out as any beginning student of yoga does, that most people don't breathe in a very healthful way either).

The wonderful thing about walking—and about this book—is its simplicity and democratic appeal. No esoterics here, no cultishness or faddishness, no artificial devices, just an incredibly simple yet powerful way to improve the quality of your life.

Maggie Spilner
Walking Editor
Prevention Magazine
December 11, 1989

CHAPTER 1

Walking and the Fitness Revolution

The political, social, sexual, cultural, and artistic revolutions of the 1960s had hardly cooled when another great revolution began. This was the Great Fitness Revolution—and it swept us all into an unprecedented change in our relationship to our bodies.

Suddenly physical fitness became available to everyone. Anyone could be a runner or an aerobic dancer or a body builder. The possibility of developing good health, maintaining good health, and enhancing our physical appearance changed forever how we live our lives.

Even as the revolution's first bastille of flab and paunch and cellulite were being stormed, many experts were recommending "modest" increases in physical exertion. Yet there was still a pervasive feeling that "more is better." The benefits of high-intensity aerobic exercise were highly touted. Milder physical activities were virtually ignored—and that included walking, which was viewed more as an exercise for recovery from disease or injury than as a "true" exercise.

Running boomed, aerobic dancing bounced, and weights became a weighty topic of conversation. Spectacular changes in the body were available to anyone willing to put in time and effort. Physical excellence was no longer the province of entertainers, athletes, or the elite. Physical excellence became the new ideal and for a while it looked like we might become a nation of amateur athletes.

The term "aerobic" had been coined by Dr. Kenneth Cooper in 1968, and by 1986 the word entered the Oxford English Dictionary where the definition read: "A method of physical exercise for producing beneficial changes in the respiratory and circulatory systems by activities which require only a modest increase in oxygen intake and so can be maintained."

But to many people "aerobics" and "modest" were seldom associated. The values of aerobic exercise were touted by physicians and fitness advocates alike, and sweeping were the claims for "aerobic fitness." If you were "out-of-shape" you might have felt left out and remained sedentary. If you were trying to get in shape, you may have felt challenged and excited by the stupendous promises and guarantees aerobic exercise seemed to promote—better health, better sex life, better relationships, better bodies, better lives—and gone back to the gym.

Running became the pre-eminent aerobic activity and by 1976, when the 2,090 New York City marathoners ran out of Central Park and into the streets of New York, the running boom was on. Jim Fixx's running book appeared on *The New York Times* bestseller list and settled in for the "long run." And those lone road runners of yesteryear, those oddities of huffing and puffing were on their way to becoming heroes. Now they were the ones masses of us wanted to emulate.

The motto of the revolution became "no pain, no gain." And the kind of pain that was most valuable was aerobic pain.

And how did you know if your discomfort was aerobic enough? Your badge of courage of sweat. Sweating became a desirable experience, an indicator that you were getting aerobic benefit from your physical efforts.

But sometime in the mid-1980s fatigue started to settle into our bones. The fatigue that fitness was supposed to remedy became the fatigue now caused by exercise. The dream of a better life through exercise was beginning to turn into a nightmare for some people. Health experts were expressing concern over an increasing number of people who were overindulging in exercise the way other people overdid food, drugs, or gambling. The result of overuse of the body were injuries such as stress fractures, shin splints, ligament and tendon inflammation—and sometimes for women cessation of their menstrual cycle.

The dark side of the exercise revolution emerged in the form of an undertone of extreme seriousness about exercise that seemed to be eroding our spirits. Even though the statistics showed yearly increases in the numbers of people exercising, there were still other statistics that showed that most exercisers were erratic in their exercise patterns, that the "sticking-with-it" factor was really the hardest part of any exercise program, and that boredom, great waves of plain boredom, were striking down exercisers faster than injuries.

Walking seldom appeared among any list of "worthwhile activities." Little attention was paid to it, and walking was viewed as a necessity rather than a vital aspect of a fitness program. The experts were neglecting the most basic exercise of all. These feet of ours may have been made for walking, but only to get you to your "real" fitness activities.

Maybe it was some weary runner; maybe it was a burnt-out aerobics enthusiast; maybe it was some stalwart grandmother who, feeling left out by the zeal of high-pitched exercisers, made walking for health visible and viable and inviting, but by mid-1985 there was more talk about walking as a satisfactory form of exercise than there had been in the entire decade and a half since the Fitness Revolution had begun.

The kind of walking that began to be touted, however, was not the kind of walking the human body was designed to do with grace. It was fast and powerful walking done at uncomfortable speeds, and brought with it something foreign to the natural movement of the body, something called "technique." Not content to let nature take its course, fitness "experts" looked into the body's mechanics and asked: How can we make walking better? "Better" meant faster, more powerful, and using more technique.

The enormous popularity of walking for exercise occurred faster than our understanding of the biomechanics of fitness walking; and, in our hunger for information and knowledge, we turned to the only source that appeared to have any technical legitimacy. Everyone drew only from that source. These new fitness walking styles were all modeled from race walking. Race walking is essentially a technical sport like gymnastics or diving. The question is not simply who crosses the finish line first, as it is in running, but who is the first walker to finish without being disqualified. Because speed is of the essence in the sport of race walking, the look of the race walker is radically different from that of any other walker. The race walker, in the pursuit of speed, hyperextends various parts of the body, especially the legs and hips and arms, thereby altering the naturally fluid look of the walking body. Some of the elements of race walking work for the "fitness walker." More of the elements do not work because of the artificial and mechanical conditions imposed on the sport of race walking to keep the athlete within the rules. But unfortunately, it is precisely from the sport of race walking that America draws most of the present walking techniques. It's no coincidence that most of the "fitness walkers" we see in America are wildly and counter-productively pumping their arms.

All this pumping and punching is aimed at one purpose: to get you to walk faster—in the belief that faster is better. Better for your heart, better for your lungs, better for your muscles, better for your mind. Since we were still hot for speed, power, and sweat, simply walking—or walking simply—was out of the question.

Walking for Life and Fitness Is No Competitive Sport

Walking for fitness is not a competitive sport. There are no judges out there checking to see that you're doing it in the officially recognized style. Walking can and should be a graceful, pleasurable activity with a uniquely inviting appeal to anyone looking for an exercise to improve, enhance, or maintain his or her physical health. But since we have all been brainwashed to some extent about what is "exercise" and what is not "exercise" we have been caught in a storm of expectations and goals and demands that tell us what is good.

Walking well is the best-looking, most graceful, rhythmical, fluid, relaxing, strength-building use of the body. For what the Fitness Revolution failed to teach us was that our bodies have their own wisdom. Each one of our bodies has its own rhythm and style, and its own natural way of achieving strength, flexibility, and relaxation.

The Body-Mind Link:
The Walking Perspective

Any person can deepen the relationship of their body to their mind through walking. Our sensitive, wholesome approach to walking can be the foundation for you to personally experience a stronger link between your body and your mind. And this link is vital to your overall health.

The body and mind communicate with each other and continually affect each other. Any system that exalts one over the other commits a gross error. Which is more important—the mind or the body—has been the focus of philosophical debate and religious thinking going back to antiquity. The great seventeenth-century philosopher René Descartes exalted the mind and vowed never to accept any idea unless he had first subjected it to rigorously critical analysis. His emphasis on the rational mind had a tremendous influence on Western thinking. Westerners tend to subordinate intuitive/feeling experience to empirical/scientific evidence.

The body certainly has the weaker reputation. It seems more a burden than a joy, being prey to illness, profound discomforts, injury, and the flux of uncontrollable and whimsical emotions. Yet the body is the very seat of life. Our body is our physical experience of life. Our senses are alive and palpable in the body. Full health is the result of a strong interaction and communication between body and mind. That strong connection is developed over time; it is not one golden moment of realization or enlightenment that is then locked into place permanently. Walking the way we advocate and teach develops both your body and your awareness of your body. This "positive walking" can be a cornerstone for a satisfying life and for good health.

As you set your physical system into motion, so your emotional/mental system will start uncramping and pent-up negative feelings can be released momentarily, even if the deep root of emotional disorder is not resolved. And that relief in the moment, which is real and substantial, can help you regain perspective. Walking with wholesome physical movement and mental awareness can forge the ongoing link between your body and your mind. And that link can be a key to good health.

The human mind has many, many layers. You cannot simply will your mind to be positive. That's the focus of the great universal debate over centuries and culture and traditions. But at the heart of all great teachings about human consciousness, lies the principle of relaxation, or "being in the moment." There are countless ways to induce this state, but we feel that positive walking is the simplest, most direct, and accessible means to call forth that exquisite state of energy, vitality, and good spirits.

Every step of the way, you can develop greater awareness and consciousness. Without the driven, pushy walking styles of the Fitness Revolution, you will tune into yourself and learn more about who you are.

We also hope to help you experience your walks as pleasurable and life-enhancing. Deep pleasure is not an escape from discomfort. It is a state of satisfaction that beckons. By learning the simple, natural moves in our book, you will open the door to an uplifting communication between your body and your mind. Step by step, minute by minute, day by day, you can experience greater balance and awareness.

CHAPTER 2

There's a Walker
in Everyone

There's a walker in everyone. Somewhere inside all of us there's a person who wants to learn more about him or herself and who senses that there's more to fitness than a healthy heart, strong muscles, and limber limbs.

We know that a positive mental attitude coupled with good physical exercise is a major key to a fulfilled life. But how do you maintain a positive mental attitude if you're engaged in an activity you don't enjoy? How do you build harmony by distorting your body's natural grace?

Letting Go of the
Harsh Technique

We met Tom at a walking clinic we conducted at a mall in Texas. Tom was sixty-three years old and appeared in robust health. He was focused on our presentation and asked numerous questions during our question-

and-answer period. He seemed especially concerned about getting his heart rate into the target heart-rate zone.

David walked with him during the mall walk and learned that Tom was a Marine Corps veteran who had married his childhood sweetheart. His youthful athleticism was fading into memory (he had been a sprinter in high school) and Tom was beginning to develop the proverbial middle-age paunch.

As the fitness craze swept the country in the early '70s Tom decided to turn to running again. His children were on their own by then, and Tom was stimulated by the sight of men his own age renewing themselves through the rigors of exercise. But his enthusiasm outdistanced his body's capacity for exercise, and he was the victim of injury after injury. He basically ignored many of the signals his body was giving him to "Slow down, Tom, take it easy, Tom," and after three years of both accomplishment and frustration and injury, he hung up his running shoes for good.

Tom was also beginning to feel the effects of his business pressures with an increase in his blood pressure and chronic tension in his neck and shoulders. His doctor prescribed medication for his blood pressure and suggested that Tom "walk off some of that steam," but Tom scoffed at the notion of walking. It seemed tame and insubstantial. Instead, Tom took up golf and became an avid player, all the time conscious that the pressure of the game and keeping below par really only fed his own tendency to feel tension. Tom had no real way to relax.

By 1986, as walking became more acceptable, recognized, and applauded as worthy exercise, Tom reconsidered his first rejection of walking. He purchased

24

some of the walking books on the market and generally sought inspiration from magazines, books, and TV. But he was very intent on turning walking into a power performance of accomplishment, complete with goals and purpose. His view of exercise was still connected to athletics, so walking seemed unchallenging and unproductive. But he did admit to himself that his own aerobic capacity and muscular conditioning were extremely limited. And maybe, just maybe, he thought, after developing some walking efficiency, he could go back to running.

To fulfill his athletic vision, Tom purchased hand, ankle, and body weights after seeing them displayed on the cover of a national magazine. Now even he wasn't so foolish as to begin saddling his body with additional pounds on his early walks. Tom set himself a schedule of three to four thirty-minute walks each week and was soon joined by several men of his age in the neighborhood. Soon, however, the Walking Buddies, as they called themselves, were also joining Tom on his weight walks. But within a short two months of starting his exercise walking regime, Tom was piling on the pounds, and his companions joined him in the great weight inflation.

Once again, all body signals of stress and distress were ignored as the Buddies got caught up in the challenges of time, distance, and poundage. Soon the distortion of the excess weight manifested as tiny muscle tears in the shoulders and a pulled muscle here and there. The troops were slowed down. They all wisely lowered their excess burdens and admitted that they had pushed too hard.

Tom was still very determined to maintain his target heart-rate goals. So as soon as one injury healed he would up the poundage again. But a tear in the muscle of his shoulder from pumping the weights really scared him and by the time we met him, he was both determined and forlorn. The Buddies had broken up as a group and his friends had generally slowed down their walking efforts.

Tom was also beginning to recognize that his ego and his male vanity were forming many of his decisions, but he couldn't seem to pull away from his self-created challenges. He just loved the challenge and went for it, even though these challenges compromised his health.

So at the mall walking clinic when Tom heard David talk about unleashing the body's natural positive power and energy without the use of anything harsh or artificial, he felt attracted to learning more. After the mall seminar David took Tom for a walk around the mall to observe Tom's body in motion. David also used the store windows as a mirror and instructed Tom to see his own reflection while walking.

David noticed that Tom had a military bearing and a marching style to his walk. Tom shared that he loved marching in the service and was a real fan of marching music, especially John Philip Sousa's. As David coached Tom he suggested that Tom relax his face by making occasional yawning movements since his jaw was tight and firm.

David instructed him to relax his chin and let his eyes travel downward a bit so that his head wasn't tilted upward. He also urged Tom to let out a sigh every now and then as a way of releasing tension. Reluctant at first, Tom grunted and let out heavy sighs; soon the release became visible on his face.

David instructed Tom to use his feet and legs more energetically, really feeling the ground as his feet moved. He also suggested that Tom use a portable cassette player on his walks and play the music he loved— those marches that encouraged his strong walking style—while learning different ways to march.

But Tom was still concerned about getting his heart rate up, so David asked him why. "Because that's why I'm exercising," said Tom, "to keep my heart healthy. I'm just following all the advice I read and hear."

"But if you keep injuring yourself by overreaching, your heart will never have a chance to develop greater efficiency," David pointed out.

"I know that, too. I guess I'm trying to make up for lost time. All those years when I didn't exercise, I keep thinking about the time I wasted. And I don't like this," he said poking his paunch with annoyance. "Too much meat and fried food, my doctor tells me. That's another hard habit to change."

During the walk Tom was like a pressure cooker letting off steam. He talked about his frustrations with himself for not reaching his goals; he talked about his injuries; he talked about his doubts that walking really could be an effective form of exercise.

And during his walking David kept making suggestions:

- don't clench your hands into fists;
- shorten your stride;
- walking briskly is not about lunging forward;
- let go of that rigid posture, drop those shoulders;
- remember you're not a soldier anymore.

Soon Tom was feeling the smoothness and rhythm of walking without the burden of weights on his limbs and torso, and the inner weight of his excessive demands on himself. Tom was pleased when he noticed that he was keeping up a good pace and that he was a little out of breath and his words were sort of slowing down. His face showed that he was relaxing, and then his body began to reflect unique strength, rhythm, and ease. At the outset of the walk Tom had protested that he had no rhythm at all, so he was surprised to feel the natural beat of his footsteps. He began to realize that he was so intense before and during his walking outings that he had no real sense of his body.

Walking from the Body's Center of Movement

As he and David kept their smooth-paced walk around the mall they were joined by other walkers who wanted to know what was going on. One woman had noticed that Tom's arms were bent at a lower angle than most of the fitness walkers around them.

She confronted David immediately. "That won't work at all," she stated adamantly. "You have to pump your arms to walk faster."

"How do you know that?" asked David.

"I read it in a book," she snapped.

"How long have you been walking for exercise?" David asked her.

"For a year, and I am definitely faster than I was when I started. It must be because I'm pumping my arms," she declared.

"Are you enjoying your walks?" David asked her. She looked at him curiously. "Are you enjoying your walks?" David asked again.

"I never thought about it that way," she answered

brusquely. Tom was still within earshot of this conversation and chuckled to himself as he recognized that he, too, had forgotten about the pleasure that comes from moving the body in a relaxed, yet strong, manner.

"Thanks for your help, David," said Tom shaking David's hand. "What you showed me really feels different to me. It's not complicated, it's real practical. Look's like you have a tough customer on your hands now. Good luck."

As David turned around, the "tough customer" extended her hand. "I'm Evelyn. I'm a bit of a skeptic. I try things for myself to see if they work. And I say that pumping arms on fitness walks works." Evelyn appeared to be a hearty woman in her late 40s. And when David asked her some questions about her exercise history she brushed him aside. "I used to be a high school gym teacher, so I know all about the body. I go for long hikes and I took up fitness walking last year. I like pumping my arms. Seems to make a lot of sense to me. I want to get that upper body working right along with my legs. Now, your wife over there, she seems to know something about how to walk gracefully, but she doesn't use her arms much so she probably can't go very fast, can she?"

David beckoned Deena, who had previously noticed Evelyn walking in the group because of her forceful footsteps. Deena told Evelyn the truth: "I'm not a speed walker and I do not 'use' walking for that purpose. I am very conscious of my physical form—posture, breathing, balance, and rhythmic grace during my walks. But I can maintain all these at faster speeds."

Evelyn felt the need to challenge Deena to a test on all this. They agreed to a little race. We set our course. David performed the "ready, set, go" honors and they set off for about fifty yards. Evelyn sprinted off, arms flailing, fists pummeling the air, energetic to be sure, but tense, tight, and constricted.

Evelyn in Motion:
- *exaggerated side-to-side arm motion*
- *unnaturally high arm swing*
- *raised shoulders*
- *stiff back*
- *carries her arms instead of letting them hang naturally*
- *tense, mechanical walk*

Deena glided in beside her, moving from her hips, shoulders relaxed, feeling that powerful foot-to-ground connection as she pushed off strongly from her heels to her toes. Evelyn's fierce determination and athletic training carried her rigid body at a respectable pace. She seemed to move by sheer force of will, aided by years of genuine muscular endurance.

As Deena glided by her in a seemingly effortless stride—body aligned, arms swinging at a moderate bend at the elbows, hips undulating—onlookers saw an incongruous picture. With all her effort and arm pumping, Evelyn should be winning; yet, there was Deena moving along, easily gaining in force and momentum to win this short contest.

Evelyn was breathless; Deena wasn't. She looked peeved and plain annoyed. "Now, just how did you manage to do that?"

Evelyn needed some pointers in walking from the body's center of movement, instead of away from it. First Deena firmly instructed her to drop her arms to her side. "Now just use your regular walking motion and each time your foot strikes the ground, really feel the ground, use it as a support. Put the emphasis on your legs and feet and let your arms move naturally, comfortably."

Evelyn complained that now she felt awkward. "I never paid any attention to my feet before. It feels strange." She seemed almost embarrassed by her awkwardness and quickly brought up her arms to cover her discomfort. Deena prodded her to drop her arms again and encouraged her to walk on an imaginary center line.

"And Evelyn," Deena said almost conspiratorially, "here's the secret of my success. Try to think of your body with a little motor driving you from your center, just a couple of inches above your belly button." Evelyn shot Deena a totally skeptical look. "Think of your-self as a wonderful racing car with a finely tuned motor that you want to use wisely and winningly."

And so Deena and Evelyn walked in tandem without pumping arms; Evelyn was starting to cruise evenly and rhythmically. She suddenly let out a spontaneous sigh, as if her breath had deepened and dropped lower, almost into her belly, and then her body moved with a grace and relaxation for just a few paces. Evelyn looked at us and smiled sheepishly. "That felt different," she first remarked. "Feels stronger," she said almost to herself. Then she asked Deena to walk with her, the same fifty yards. She shifted the emphasis from her arms to her legs, and as we continued our walk we were joined by other walkers.

Soon Evelyn was getting the rhythm in her hips and legs. Her knowledge and athletic skills were helping her now. As she felt and looked more comfortable, some of her peers kidded her and she was soon laughing, being a good sport. Evelyn confessed that she had always been a fierce competitor and that she had brought that same attitude to her fitness walking. Now she could evaluate that there was another dimension to walking; she had felt it for herself. And then she sprinted directly to the end of the corridor and back, her arms high and aggressive. That was a part of Evelyn, too. We could see that she had learned some balance between the effort of her upper and lower body and that she looked more comfortable and graceful.

Both Tom and Evelyn were looking to improve their general level of health and well-being. In their drive and intensity, however, they had both overlooked the factor of enjoyment and pleasure. And while each had come to walking as an alternative to strenuous physical exertion, they each brought a certain quality of harshness to their walking.

When we added in the magic ingredients of enjoyment, relaxation, rhythm, and balance, they both felt the change in their bodies from a driven walk to the dance of walking. The lightness and freeing energy they both experienced translated itself into the speed they wanted plus fluidity and an uncomplicated state of relaxation.

Since both of them were concerned about developing and maintaining sufficient aerobic capacity they were extremely pleased to find that they could accelerate their respective walking speeds through a more harmonious and natural series of walking movements.

The next chapter will explain what they learned in our walking clinic.

CHAPTER 3

The Walking Clinic—
The Balboa
Walking Approach

The steps in this chapter will get you to walk well at *any* speed. They are effective for your everyday walking, for your cross-training, and even for race walking. They will teach you how to walk faster by accelerating naturally and how to walk slower by decelerating naturally. Your body will not suffer from strain or injury.

As with any exercise program, you should check with your doctor before beginning our walking approach.

Technique: The "Steps"

The word has a forbidding sound when we think of walking. Most of us associate technique with dance, music, acting. All specialized physical activities rely in some way on the development of skill and technique particular to that activity.

Walking is *not* a specialized action. Neither is it a

sport. Yet, at the same time, we are firmly and certainly committed to a need for everyone to become more adept at walking. A contradiction? Not at all. Our approach is based on discovering and utilizing the inherent wisdom of your body's own biomechanics. Rather than overlaying an assortment of artificial and manipulated moves, we are generating movements that unlock, release, and enhance your inborn skill of walking. These movements can and will bring you into an awareness of your body and feelings that you may never have experienced, regardless of how adept you may be at other physical activities.

Walking, fundamental though as it is to our nature, can be developed into an art. So we present you now with these "steps," a jostling of your body's memory system to help it regain some of the animation, lightness and playfulness of your childhood.

These are the steps to help your steps become lighter and brighter.

1. The Walking Center—the Line

Imagine a straight line going down the road or pathway. This line represents your center, the center of your body or just the center, a benchmark by which you measure your walk. You can use a wide line already painted on the road if you wish. Walk with your normal stride and aim to plant your feet close to the line and parallel to it. Your feet should not cross the line, however, your toes should point straight ahead.

2. Gliding Effortless Motion

Start by walking smoothly with a gliding effortless motion. Feel a sense of lightness to your steps. You can imagine that you have on a pair of roller skates or a pair of ice skates. Really feel that gliding motion. Try to avoid over- and understriding. Find a comfortable stride length that feels good to you. You can tell if you are overstriding by the fact that your head feels like it is going up and down or bobbing with each step.

3. Heel to Toe

When race walking and other versions of fast walking started at the turn of this century, they were referred to as "heel-toe." Essentially the motion in the walk is related to landing your feet on the heel and rolling to the toe area and pushing off. Much like a rocker.

Heel to toe is an important concept and motion that applies very well to today's walking methods. It also helps you feel and touch the earth by rolling your feet gently from heel to toe. It's important here to mention that in order to feel the earth and have it support you, you should not slap the earth on its face. Yes, don't slap the earth!

It is normal for everybody to land their feet with their heels first and almost everybody then lets the foot drop and "slap" the earth without going through the gentle roll to the toes. So for most people it's heel landing and "slap" the ground with the rest of the foot. In order for the "slap" not to occur, a little muscle effort is required. You have to flex the foot, or in simple terms, you have to keep the foot up and let it roll gently to the toes.

That flexing of the foot can cause what some walkers feel as shin pain. This usually happens in the initial stages of strengthening the shin muscle. It is important to strengthen the shin muscle since it is, in simple

Flexing your foot:
Heel to toe helps you by rolling your feet gently from heel to toe.
Nearly everybody plants their feet with their heels first and then
lets the foot drop and "slap" the earth without going through the
gentle roll to the toes. In order for the "slap" not to occur, you
have to flex the foot, or in simple terms, you have to keep the
foot up and let it roll gently to the toes. Maintain that heel-to-toe
motion for the feet after you plant them. The action is similar to
that of a rocker and creates a gentle straightening of the legs.

terms, the opposite member, or antagonist, of the very
powerful calf muscle.

For walkers who feel this shin pain, you can tilt your
foot slightly to the outside edge of the shoe and make
the transition from the heel to the toe. In most in-
stances this will ease some of the shin pain experienced until you build strength in them. This might take
months, depending on how weak they are, so do not be

discouraged if the discomfort persists. As you walk for a mile or two, the twinge will usually subside. If not, then stop and stretch your shins.

This muscle imbalance between the front of the leg and the back of the leg has created much pain for many runners in the form of shin splints and pain. Many runners have imbalances of these two muscles, with the shins being the weak link. (Runners could do themselves a great service by balancing out their leg muscles with a little cross-training by fitness walking.) Walkers generally develop a better equality in strength of these two muscle groups because of the more balanced motion of walking.

So by flexing the foot, you establish that gentle roll from heel to toe. Maintain that strong heel-to-toe motion for the feet after you plant them. The action is similar to that of a rocker and creates a gentle straightening of the legs. And for you aerobics participants, you could say this is like a leg-lift in motion. As you develop this strong foot and leg action you will engage every muscle of your hips and backside to create that beautiful firm line that is so admired.

Another powerful image to help you find support from the ground or the earth is that of feeling the earth. We said that earlier, but let's be even more specific now. Try to think of your foot as your hand. What your hand is to your arm, your foot can be to your leg. And just as your hand is there sensitively feeling, touching, and moving objects about without a thought, so, too, can your foot be an instrument of touch and feel and motion.

The motion part we all just do; it's automatic. But if you were to actually use your foot to slowly, sensually, deliberately feel the ground—letting your foot roll evenly forward to touch the earth and grab each inch so that you get a strong feel for the ground all across the sole of your foot—then something quite astonishing happens. As your foot, the foundation of your body, makes that strong contact, your entire body straightens more—is supported and strengthened by this base we call earth—and you are lifted and carried and helped to walk by this earth of ours. Just taking some time to acquaint yourself with this easy, surprising touch—even at home, a very good place to practice— will bring you into contact with a superb action.

The rewards are: beautiful posture without artificially pulling your body upright; strong alignment as you feel both feet individually (and maybe for the first time) make contact with the ground; release of tension from the upper body and the lower back as you allow the ground to support and lift you instead of trying to hold yourself up; great-looking legs which are being "exercised" every time you walk; a natural strengthening of your tummy muscles, again because you are being supported by the earth instead of fighting gravity, which causes a range of physical distortions; the natural development of a sense of presence and poise because you will allow yourself to be conscious and present, instead of the rushing or "spaced-out" quality that too many of us live in; a deepening of your breathing, which will create a sense of peace and relaxation and calm.

And all this can come from simply touching, feeling, and being supported by the earth!

4. Foot Placement

If you toe-out normally, try to compensate by gently bringing your feet to walk parallel to the line. If you toe-in naturally, try to place your feet parallel to your line of travel. This effort to make your feet travel that straight and narrow path will result in proper body alignment and good carriage. It will make the entire walking gait easier to accomplish. When the feet are flared out, as they generally are for average walkers, it is harder for them to mobilize and turn the hip as they walk. The ducklike walk creates a waddle effect. If you do have very flared-out feet, just try to aim them toward that direction of travel. Don't force them to be parallel. It takes time for the body to adjust and you might be able to make only a slight adjustment in the angle of your feet, and that's enough to get you on your way.

Foot Placement

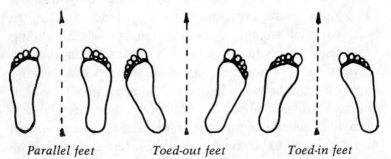

Parallel feet   *Toed-out feet*   *Toed-in feet*

Proper foot placement is a critical area for achieving a fluid walking style. Try to concentrate on achieving as parallel a foot placement as you can muster. Again, experiment with toeing-in and toeing-out, and you will feel how maintaining parallel feet can facilitate proper alignment and help you toward your goal of a more beneficial walking style.

It is important to note that as your walking speed increases, your feet should land closer and closer to that center line. As you slow down, you will note that your feet land farther and farther from the line.

5. The Back Leg

With respect to the ground supporting you, another important point here is to have you maintain the back leg and foot on the ground for an instant longer than you are accustomed to. And really feel the push-off with the foot. Letting the back leg maintain that longer contact facilitates hip rotation and will add strength to your posture and power to your walk.

6. The Foot and Leg Motion

Once again—feel the ground with your feet. Feel the ground from the heel of the foot as it rolls firmly to the toe. Feel the feet press into the earth and feel the ground supporting you.

To help visualize the proper leg and foot motion, we will now look closely at the stride. In all forms of walking, the stride has two phases: the swing phase and support phase. During the swing phase, the leg is off the ground and moving forward. Here the muscles are relaxed and you can see that the leg is bent at the hip, the knee, and the ankle.

As your foot nears the ground, your leg straightens slightly and is then actually bent slightly at impact. Your foot will touch the ground well back on your heel with toes up (flexing the ankle and not letting the foot slap forward), and then the foot rolls forward to your toes. Feel the earth, let the earth support you. So once the foot touches the earth, your leg is in the support phase and will gently straighten. Rolling forward over the supporting leg maintains your forward momentum.

41

As your body passes over your straightened leg, you now move into the most important part of the support phase. The major source of power of forward motion in fitness walking comes from pushing off with the calf muscles through the toe push-off (plantar flexion for anatomists). To maximize the power of your stride, you need to concentrate on driving forward, not upward, all the way through to the toe-off.

Your feet should be tracking parallel to the center line. Heel to toe, heel to toe. The hips are swinging in their up and down, forward and backward, to and fro motion. Not from side to side. This side-to-side motion of the hips, though, is seen in many dance steps.

The hips and their rotation are giving you those extra few inches of stride length and making it easier for you to walk with ease and grace and fluidity. Imagine your legs lengthening by starting their motion at your walking center. The feeling you get from this motion, once practiced, is very close to the dance of life.

7. Longer Legs

By initiating the action of the legs from your center, you should note that the knees and legs are tracking parallel and straight ahead. Walking parallel to that center line achieves that added stride length by rotation of the hip toward that center line. All these motions you have done before, and now you are adding just a little more rotation to your hips to get that added stride length. So in essence, you are increasing your stride by rotating the hips instead of trying to take a longer step just with your legs.

Visualize and imagine your legs beginning a few inches above the belly button and your movement will become smoother and much more energetic. You will start to develop a smoother gliding action—not a lifting action—of the leg.

This is based on the actual muscle that connects your lower spine to the pelvis and to the legs. This core muscle, the psoas (see Chapter Six), is real and this motion is real.

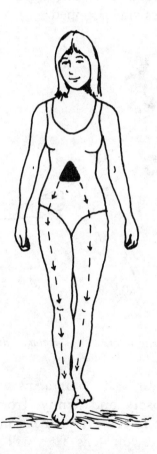

Longer Legs
Visualize and imagine your legs beginning a few inches above the belly button (the center of movement) and you will start to develop a smoother gliding action, not a lifting action, of the leg.

8. Shoulders and Arms

Shoulders should be relaxed and dropped. Allow arms to swing naturally in counterbalance to the legs, just as you do in your normal everyday walk. Just let your arms hang loosely from the shoulder sockets. Relax your shoulders. Let the arms hang; *do not try to carry them.* Again it's very important to let the arms hang so that the shoulders stay dropped.

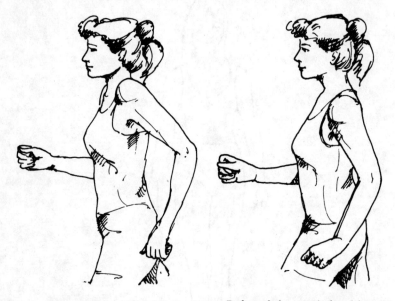

Hunched-up shoulders   *Relaxed dropped shoulders*

As you begin to walk, your arms will swing all by themselves, loosely and firmly, from the shoulder socket. Without intervention, the arms will swing in counterbalance to your legs. They will swing according to your own style and body without your ever giving that movement any effort.

9. The Backward Arm Swing

Emphasize the backswing more than the forward swing. Simply feel it go further back than normal, and without affecting the frontswing. This will facilitate the counter-rotation of the hip in a very helpful way. It will increase the range of motion in the hips, and that backward stretch of the hips is a fundamental function of walking well.

The Counterrotation and Torque of Your Body
The twisting and turning around the axis (the spine) of the body.
The shoulders turn one way, the hips turn and rotate the other
way in counterbalance to each other.

This backswing of the arm works to align the spine squarely over the legs. The backswing of the arms creates the proper counter-rotation for the hips to rotate forward with greater ease. It reduces the inclination to have that forward-body lean.

The backswing allows the body to stay erect and provides time for the back leg to stay on the ground longer, giving you a greater push-off from your toes. So again relax the shoulders and carry your arms low. The arms can be slightly bent at the elbow. The elbow can be firm but not locked in that position. The arm should be swung as one unit, with no flapping around. Feel the energy of the arm as being one unit, solid yet relaxed and mobile.

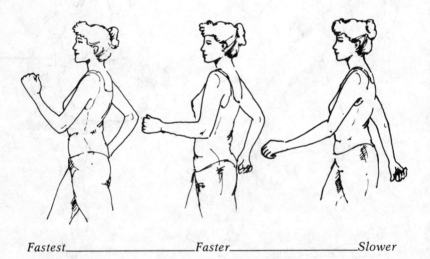

Fastest_____Faster_____Slower

Your arm bend is proportionate to your walking speed.
As you accelerate your walking, the elbow arm angle will change body to compensate for the speed. Keep the angle of the elbow firm as the arm swings back and forth. The bend at the elbow should be proportionate to your walking speed.

Find the elbow arm angle where you feel the most relaxation and rhythm. Try a variety of arm angles until you do. It is important for you to note that when you accelerate your walking, the elbow arm angle will be changed by your body almost automatically to compensate for the speed. If you allow it, that is. So let the wisdom of the body govern this motion and merely observe and allow it to happen. Keep the angle of the elbow firm and do not open and close the angle as the arm swings back and forth. *The bend at the elbow should be proportionate to your walking speed.*

10. Arm Swing

As your arm swings, allow the elbows to skim your body. You will generally feel your thumb brush the sides of the hips as a good indicator that your elbows are held in.

Your forward arm swing should not go higher than your breast line and your backward swing should go no further than your buttocks. Keep the arms low and dropped throughout the full range of motion.

Let the shoulders swing back and forth just a little with each swing. A rigid torso and shoulders take up a lot of work—so let your upper body dance and sway with the natural undulations of the walk.

Pay special attention to the hunching and tensing of the shoulders as you experiment with bent arm angles. Make sure that your shoulders are dropped and relaxed while you bend your arms. This is a particularly tricky area to be aware of. Many walkers seem to assume that tension and rigidity in the hunched shoulders are normal feelings when the arm is bent. This is not so and experimentation and awareness will get you that sense of flow and rhythm without any tension.

The direction of the arm swing should be noted. By using the dial of a clock as a reference, you will feel that swinging the left arm from 12 o'clock to 7 o'clock would be close to ideal. (Twelve o'clock is directly ahead of the body.) By swinging the right arm in the direction of the travel within 12 o'clock in front and 5 o'clock in back will keep you in good form.

Swinging the arms too much across the body will throw off your balance and center of gravity. You will

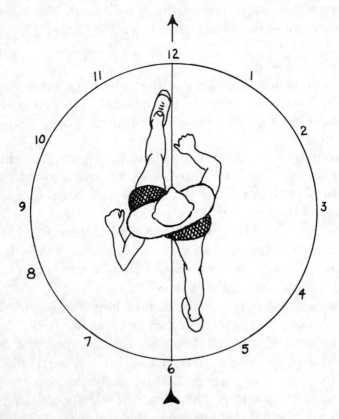

The dial of a clock for giving directions:
Use of the dial of a clock to give accurate directions as to the swing of the arms.

have to use a great deal of force to keep yourself centered and walking that line. Otherwise you will weave in and out as if you were a drunken driver. Walking is a natural event. Diverting from the natural does not feel right or do justice to Mother Nature.

11. The Hip Rotation
In order for the foot to be placed close to that line,

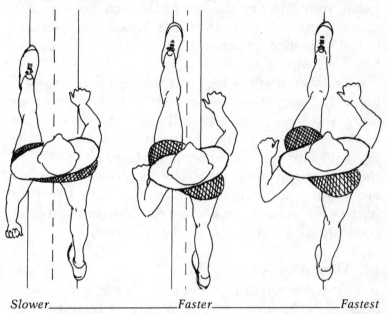

Slower_____Faster_____Fastest

Hip Rotation
As you increase your walking speed, allow the hips to gently rotate forward toward the direction of travel. Gently aim and turn the sides of your hip toward that center line to facilitate the rotation. As you begin to increase your walking speed, your hips will rotate even more in their range of motion. You will note that as your speed increases, your feet will land closer and closer to that center line. The upper body, the torso, and especially the arms act as the counterbalancing partners for the hips and lower body. To walk faster, allow your hips to set the rhythm and speed.

allow the hips to rotate forward gently as the leg is extended to achieve that slightly longer stride than the one you normally use in your everyday walking.

Gently aim and turn the sides of your hip toward that center line to facilitate the rotation and the motion. Aim for a dancelike freedom in the hips. Now, as you have read throughout this book, your hips rotate as you walk. As you begin to increase your walking speed, your hips are likely to rotate even more in their range of motion. This rotation is normal and pleasant to feel and will be experienced as very natural once you become aware of it.

Remember that the legs and the hips are the workhorse and propulsion motor for the body. The upper body, the torso, and especially the arms act as the counterbalancing partners. The work is done by the legs and hips and no amount of vigorous flapping of the arms is going to get you to move faster—unless you are in water and swimming. *To walk faster, allow your hips to set the rhythm and speed.* Your arms are not constructed by nature to set that function.

12. The Shoulders

Here it is important that you feel you are leading your body with the hips and not by leaning forward with your torso. This allows the torso to ride in the pelvic girdle by sitting squarely and well balanced and assisting in the ride. We see so many people hunching and bunching their shoulders forward as if to propel themselves forward by their upper torso. Bent on going faster—faster than they are able—they try to compensate for their "slowness" by angling themselves forward. This throws their entire body off-balance and actually slows them down. Speed is not always of the essence, and if it's speed you want then only time and continual, efficient walking will build the stamina and muscle strength that eventually produce fluid speed.

13. The Hands

Keep hands closed softly as if you were carrying soft cotton. Keep hands in a straight line and symmetrical with the wrists. Do not let the hand be limp or dangling or flapping about. Limp hands create pooling of blood and lymphatic fluids. You will note that limp hands swell a lot after a walk. By keeping the hands in line

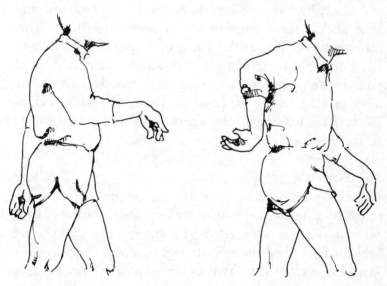

Limp Hands
Limp hands will lead to distortion in the shoulders by forcing the arms to carry them. Limp hands interfere with proper alignment of the arm and throughout the torso. Try to keep your hands aligned with your wrist and the rest of the arm. Keep hands softly cupped.

with the arm, the pooling of fluids will be at a minimum.

Limp hands will lead to distortion in the shoulder girdle because you will be made to carry the hands as if you are carrying a limp piece of meat. It sets off imbalances in the whole shoulder and arm carriage and the shoulders will rise in order to carry them—thus, stress on the system begins. The hands softly closed, with the thumb on top, will give the most effective position for the swing of the arm.

You will energize the hand and arm with a correct alignment. It will pay off with a better rhythm, better posture, better image, and better energy. Limp hands are out, aligned arm and hands are in. The hand and arm should be swinging as an integrated unit. This alignment of the hands is a very important feature of the body-mind connection with such a large chunk of your brain's gray matter having control over the hand. Making a fist is the other no-no with the hands. A tight fist creates tension in the arms and that is transmitted to the rest of the body.

14. The Jaw
Slacken your jaw by yawning or opening the mouth wide, by uttering a grunt or two, or a sigh or two. Much tension will be released with a softer jaw. You should feel the easing of tension throughout your body as your jaw relaxes. A full yawn is an excellent way to ease tension out of the body.

15. The Head
Try to keep your head squarely on top of the shoulders and in line with the rest of the body. Easier said than

done. Pay attention to the position of the head or have someone relay the information to you on how you hold it.

A Brief Summary of the Balboa Walking Approach

1. Imagine a center line going down the road or pathway. Walk with your normal stride and plant your feet *parallel* to the line. As your speed increases, your feet should land progressively closer to the center line.

2. In order for the foot to be planted close to center line, allow the hips to turn forward toward the line as the leg is extended forward.

3. *Feel the ground with your feet. Maintain that strong heel-to-toe motion of the feet after you plant them. Feel the ground from the heel of the foot as it rolls firmly to the toe. This action creates a gentle straightening of the legs at the knee.*

4. Walk as smoothly as possible, trying to sustain a gliding, effortless motion. Maintain and extend the back leg and foot on the ground for an instant longer than you are accustomed to. Feel the push-off with the foot through the toes. Letting the back leg extend and maintain contact with the ground facilitates the hip rotation and will add alignment to your posture and power to your walk.

5. Find a comfortable stride length that feels good to you. When you begin to accelerate your walk your body will shift to *shorter and faster steps,* if you don't interrupt this natural adjustment. Remember, your body has a mind and an intelligence of its own. Let the hips and legs set the rhythm and pace. Let your body do the walking and let your thinking, reasoning mind just rest for a change.

6. When you start your walk, imagine your legs beginning a few inches above the belly button. Your leg will seem longer, your movement smoother, and you will start to develop a gliding action—not a lifting action—of the leg. Your posture will automatically improve and correct itself with this motion. Keep practicing this visualization and action, which work together.

7. Shoulders should be relaxed and dropped. Do not try to carry your arms as if you are carrying a package. Allow arms to swing naturally in counterbalance to the legs, just as you do in your normal everyday walk. Emphasis should be on the backward swing, not the forward swing.

8. Keep hands closed softly as if you were carrying soft cotton. Keep hands in a straight line with the wrists.

9. Let your arms hang naturally with a slight bend at the elbow. The elbow should be held securely but not locked in that position. Keep the angle of the elbow firm and do not open and close the angle as the arm swings back and forth. *The bend at the elbow should be proportionate to your walking speed.* As your arm swings back and forth, allow the elbows to skim your body.

10. Remember that good posture always contains the possibility for movement. Good posture is not "standing at attention." It is always in dynamic balance. It is not static. Your torso should be centered in your hip girdle, sitting well-balanced, assisting in the walk with the counterbalancing swing of the arms.

11. To walk faster, allow your hips and legs to set the rhythm and speed. *Do not* try to walk faster by forcing the arms to set the pace or swing faster than the legs. Aim for a dancelike rhythmic freedom in the hips.

CHAPTER 4

Liberate Your Hips!

Our culture has something against hip movement and tries its best to teach us to keep our hips rigid when walking. The only time we're allowed the least little bit of hip movement is when we're dancing or using the fondly remembered Hula Hoop.

That's not the way it should be! The hips are part of the biomechanical design of the body—and they're designed to swing and undulate when the body walks or runs, not just when it dances. Watch joggers. With the majority of joggers you will see hardly any motion in the hip. They just seem to twist their torsos. Their bodies are like pogo sticks pounding the ground. If you understand the way the body works, you can understand why injuries are rampant. No upper body strength is achieved, and generally the legs are strong only in the back (calves and hamstring) and weak in front (quadriceps and shins). This muscle unbalancing pulls the body out of alignment and, when the stress of running is added, injury occurs.

But even if there is no injury, their faces tell a story of agony and strain. We cringe when we see this and wonder about the damage those bodies are taking. It might sound like we're against jogging, but we're not. We would just like to ask joggers to be a little more aware that the activity can have a benefit in all aspects of their lives and not just cardiovascular fitness.

The same goes for walkers, for walkers commit the same biomechanical crimes that joggers do. We don't see as many injuries in walkers because walking is, in and of itself, less stressful than jogging. And thank goodness for that, because if it were not, we'd be a nation of walking wounded! But just because walkers don't suffer the injuries joggers do doesn't mean that they don't throw the body out of alignment and do more subtle, long-term damage—physically and psychologically.

A Separate Life from the Body

As mimes have always known, a man's body movements are as personal as his signature, and as novelists have always known, body movements often reflect who a character is, we all seem to know that the way we move tells the world who we are. As a result—we try to stifle any form of self-expression that might sneak out when we're walking. What have we got against self-expression?

The most difficult aspect we have to deal with in teaching our approach is hip rotation. Oh those hips! Some of the largest and most important muscles of the body are in the hips, and moving them—or, rather, not

57

moving them—can be the source of serious problems for both men and women.

The hips, pelvis, or pelvic girdle—whatever you choose to call it—is one of the most important joints in the body. It's meant to move, it's meant to rotate in an undulating motion. It rotates for men and it rotates for women. Women have a larger hip girdle and usually exhibit a larger rotation. But men's hips move too. In walking, everyone needs to move their hips!

Of course, the actual degree of rotation depends on the speed of movement. The pelvic rotation is the single most important element of movement that separates regular walking from fast walking.

Freedom—Parole Your Hips

The ease and fluidity of the pelvis freed from its cultural prison, freed from years of restraint, freed from years of self-consciousness, freed from years of neglect can be a source of enormous power and energy to the walker. After most of the women we coach learn to move their hips, rotate their hips as they are meant to move, we always get two responses from them. First, they invariably comment that either their religion or culture had always prohibited the hips to be that free. The second response, usually stated immediately after the first, is that it feels very natural and fluid to walk that way.

When people first begin to feel the movements of the hip, they tend to feel they are overswinging them in a provocative or profane manner. You may feel slightly naughty. But don't worry. If you could see yourself on

videotape, as most of our clients do, you would see that rather than appearing naughty, your walking movement is actually quite flowing and natural—not forced at all. The fact is that when your hips are finally liberated, the feeling of freedom is actually a lot more pronounced than the appearance of it. You will feel more motion down there than is actually visible to the onlooker.

Walking as if there was a solid block between the torso and the legs is the norm in our culture, but the rear end, your fanny, your tush, your derriere whatever you want to call it—needs to be moved. For women especially, whose girth is usually around the legs and hips, it becomes imperative that the hips be used in the way nature designed them to move. Walking with the hips undulating in their glory can tone, trim, tighten, and treat you to a beautiful body. A naturally moving pelvis is able to swing freely forward and backward while walking with an easy to-and-fro motion.

Be aware, too, that a lifetime of holding the hips rigidly while walking also means there may be psychological and emotional issues bound in there with all that tightness. Liberating your hips from the rigidity may help you become free and aware in more ways than the purely physical. Most of our clients come to us because of the emphasis on walking as the vital component of reaching greater self-knowledge. They come because both body and inner life are developing.

___ CHAPTER 5 ___

What to Do
With Those Arms

The use of the arms for "fitness" walking is an area
fraught with misinformation and ignorance. Walkers
who have followed the various schools of advice and
teachings have become unwitting exponents of awkward walking styles, poor posture, stressful gaits, and
very unflattering body language.

A kinesiologist (study of human movement) and spe-
cialist in walking at Columbia University's Teachers
College in New York, Tracey M. McCullough, has been
a consultant to The Walking Center of New York City
for several years. She is currently a scientific advisor
to the United States Women's Race Walking Team and
does research for TAC/Olympic Committee for Wom-
en's Race Walking. In an attempt to counter some of
the misinformation regarding the role of the arms in
walking, she shared the following facts in a private
communication:

"As of the present date, locomotion research for hu-

man walking does not support in any way the general notion that the arms play any major role in propelling the body forward.

On the contrary, the arms primarily serve to keep the torso dynamically balanced over the pelvis while in motion. This makes common and intuitive sense given that we can move forward in walking thanks to the ground pushing up and forward against our foot during toe-off. Compare this to the insignificant mass of air flowing past the arms as we swing them.

Unfortunately, neither scientific research nor intuitive sense have yet come to the aid of the beginner walker, who more often than not has very weak musculature in the pelvis and legs. Thus, to make up for this "propulsive deficit" (the inability to walk faster because of underused, undeveloped muscles), they try to increase their forward speed by driving the arms harder and faster.

Concentrating on arm action instead of leg action, however, has three major detrimental consequences— all of which ultimately slow the walker down in one way or another. First, the synchronous coupling of arms and legs (the natural rhythmic coordinated movements of the arms and legs) is eliminated, and this condition essentially disconnects the torso from the pelvis. The body in this state moves as if it were two separate pieces, thus leading to an extremely tiresome and uncoordinated walking motion. Secondly, driving the arms harder, significantly increases tension in the rib cage and upper spine, affecting proper breathing and posture. This tension is then transferred down the spinal column and into the hips. Rather than relaxing, this tension increases spinal curvature in the lumbar spine *which often leads to lower-back problems. Finally, the overemphasis on arm action thrusts the upper spine forward, creating a walking pattern where the rib cage leads ahead of the pelvis and legs (an unnatural forward-body lean). This distortion in posture plays havoc with muscular imbalances between the upper and lower body."*

The arms should move at the same speed as the legs and it is a *myth* that the arms should move faster than the legs. Walking with rhythm and grace does *not* mean trying to force your body to move faster by vigorously swinging your arms bent at a ninety-degree angle. It does *not* mean using your arms as accelerators to force the legs to keep up with them.

This bent-arm-swing misunderstanding came out of race walking technique, which works well for that highly technical sport but works poorly for the average walker. Pumping your arms that way throws off your posture and can be hurtful. At the very least, it looks bad and doesn't make it any easier for you to enjoy your body.

Observe walkers who were told to pump their arms. They actually look as if they are in the process of pumping air into a tire of some sort. The motion is identical. Our brain can literally translate that instruction into an actual movement. It will serve you well to save your pumping for your bicycle tire and not for your walking. So, when you start out, walking slowly, just let your arms hang loosely from the shoulder sockets. Relax your shoulders. That means that you let the arms hang; *do not try to carry them.* It's very important to let the arms hang so that the shoulders stay dropped.

As you begin to walk, your arms will swing all by

themselves, smoothly, from the shoulder socket. Without thinking about them, the arms will swing in counterbalance to your legs. They will swing according to your own style and body and in the way you have been moving them all your life, without ever giving that movement a thought.

As the right leg steps forward, the left arm swings forward of its own accord. As your left leg swings backward, the right arm swings backward. You have done that all your life. The arms and shoulders move and swing in counterbalance to your legs and hips. They know how to do it without your thinking about it. The arms naturally will bend—but just a little!—as you speed up.

When you are in a hurry, your stride will quicken and your arms will start to increase the bend at the elbow to accommodate your speed. Again, the bend at the elbow will be proportionate to your walking speed. The body does that all by itself, having mastered the art of walking over years of practice.

As you reach the speeds of the faster fitness walker, your arms might—and we stress MIGHT!—be bent at about the ninety-degree angle. But it is wrong to start with a ninety-degree bent elbow if your speed is slow. If you allow yourself to trust the wisdom of your body, your body will adjust that angle of the arm very adequately according to your walking speed. What we have noticed is that to start walking by bending your arms at a right angle *actually slows you down*. It is unnatural, counterproductive, biomechanically incorrect and distorts your body and rhythm.

When running/jogging came on the fitness scene years ago there were basically no instructions about how to use legs or arms. For the most part, runners were told to just let the body do naturally what the body knows how to do. The body knows how to create the proper counterbalance for increased leg speed. So why, if there were basically no instructions for arms during running or jogging, would there be such a specific instruction for speedier walking? The body works the same way when building speed through running or walking.

The answer: It's easier to tell someone to pump their arms in order to walk faster than to lead them through the time-consuming process of learning to walk faster the natural, balanced way. There's a little urgent, impatient child in each of us that wants results instantly and that child, with its demands for instant gratification, wants results now! I want to walk faster immediately, it demands. And it's that voice that usually mucks up the process of developing strength, endurance, and speed by simply using your body naturally and wholesomely and beautifully to walk faster. And it's that voice that could even believe that pumping your arms will make you walk faster.

The Arms in Phase With the Legs

Let us state this again and again. The arms should move at the same speed as the legs. It is a myth that the arms should move faster than the legs. Many articles and books have tried to make the point that in order to make the legs go faster, you should swing your arms faster and the legs will follow. Your body will not like it. Your nervous system will not like it. It will throw your rhythm off. This myth has been disproved by exercise physiologists who have conducted studies with elite athletes. But the myth still persists. If you try to move your arms faster than your legs, you will get confused. Your body will get confused. Your limbs will be out of phase. You will end up with strange body language and a nervous system that will wonder what the heck you are trying to do to it.

In his research paper presented at the United States Olympic Committee/TAC Elite Conference in Colorado Springs in 1986, Ralph Mann, PhD., states that "if you want to improve sprint speed, *develop the strength, speed, and mechanics of the legs.* Every comparison we have made points to the conclusion that the legs are the weak link in sprinting, while the arms are only limited to moving as fast as the legs allow. *Improve leg speed and the arms will keep pace. The opposite simply is not the case.* If everyone here stood up and pumped their arms back and forth as fast as possible, virtually everyone could match the arm speed of Carl Lewis (U.S. and Olympic track champion.) None of us, however could match his tremendous leg speed" ("A Biomechanical Analysis of Sprinters," *Track Technique,* Winter 1986).

Truth: Let the legs and hips set the rhythm. Emphasize the leg and hip swing first, not the arm swing. The legs and hips have the largest and strongest and bulkiest muscles in the body. Let the arms follow the legs. Let the arms assist the legs. The arms and shoulders are far smaller and serve in a counterbalancing role. This myth creates what we call "stresswalking."

Characteristics of Stresswalking

Stresswalking has certain characteristics that seem to show up in all the persons trying to walk that way. Visually, it looks like a small child trying to appear three times bigger than he really is by pumping his arms and swaggering. Sometimes it looks as if the walker's lower body were stuck in a gooey substance and the walker was trying to fight his way out by wildly swinging the arms.

There is a top-bottom split at about the waistline. The top-half of the body seems to be at odds with what the bottom-half is doing: The top-half is trying to reach for the heavens and the bottom is holding on trying to make some sort of contact with the ground and not succeeding too well. Not only does this unbalance the body, but it renders it biomechanically unstable, too.

It looks as though the mind is trying to force the body into something it's not willing to do, with the arms dragging this reluctant body for its walk. When the lower body resists moving as fast as the arms would have it go, the arm walker bends the body at the waist and tries to push the torso ahead of it. It's as if the upper body is trying to go at a faster speed than the lower-half and since the lower-half is not cooperating, the upper-half decided to leave it behind and go ahead. But since they are joined at the waist that's an impossibility, thus the dragging image.

It gets even more exaggerated if a person is carrying weights in his hands. The weights pull the upper body forward and over, putting even more stress on the back. Then the feet start to flair out in a ducklike fashion,

67

adding to the overall dissipation of the energy and momentum.

Here is one of David's experiences which further illustrates the misconceptions surrounding the correct approach to walking:

I was on the track doing my workout and watching an older woman strugging at walking with her arms bent up high. She was moving slowly, obviously impeded by her awkward style. I felt bad for her and asked what she was trying to do. She said that she was new to walking and that she just read an article in the newspaper on walking. The article instructed the reader to walk with the arms bent at a ninety-degree angle.

Well, this woman stated that if the national newspaper said you do it this way, it must be right. I did not argue the point with her and suggested she try a little experiment with me. At first she resisted taking advice from this stranger, so I showed her my "credentials." I handed her my flyer about our work with the title "Are You a Stresswalker" from *Prevention Magazine* and that seemed to give me enough credibility with her to challenge the newspaper.

When she lowered her arms and emphasized her hip rotation and let the arms assist the movement—lo and behold, I heard the now famous exclamation—"that feels good and natural—it's easy."

I smiled and said yes, thinking I had an instant convert. But then she added, "This feels so good and easy—will I get an aerobic workout with it?"

Even though she was tense and tight from the

other walking style, she believed that tension and hardness were necessary for an aerobic workout. Ease and fluidity were foreign to her and did not coincide with the bad habit she was starting to learn from this newspaper article.

I worked with her for a while and she began to integrate the new pointers and to honor the good feeling she was starting to experience. It felt good to her, and when she tried to do her old style it did not resonate with her anymore.

We parted ways after ten minutes, with her promising to remember what she had learned and to try to *trust the feelings in her body.*

Another convert to feeling good in the body, and a decent aerobic lift in the process.

Feel the Effects of Stresswalking for Yourself

If you see a walker whose chest is up, whose shoulders are raised and brows furrowed and want to know what this attitude signifies, assume the attitude. Gulp in some air, raise your shoulders, lift your brows, and if you are in touch with your body you will immediately perceive that you have adopted an expression of fear and tension and stress. You can now understand that in the language of the body of this walker, the walker is saying, "I am afraid. I feel tense and stressed."

These chronic holding and tension patterns become so habitual that the body attitude literally becomes part of the walker's character. Since the person is unaware of the fear in his body expression, he might re-

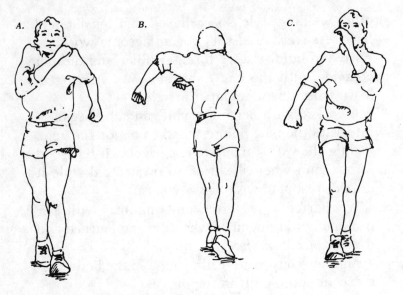

Three examples of stresswalking:
A. • *shoulders hunched up around the ears*
   • *exaggerated arm motion*
   • *pumping arms in an attempt to go faster*
   • *tense and awkward body image*

B. • *flailing the arms exaggeratedly from side to side*
   • *hunched up and rounded shoulders*
   • *mechanical and unrhythmic walking style*

C. • *punching hands in the air*
   • *unnecessarily high arm action*
   • *making fists*
   • *rigid, mechanical walk*

sort to some compensatory body attitudes such as exaggerated aggressiveness to cover the underlying attitude of fear. So you'll see him walking with an agressive style and a fierce and threatening look on his face. This phenomenon is seen time and time again on the faces and bodies of walkers with their bent arms pumping away, their chests raised, shoulders hunched, and an expression of discomfort and apprehension on their faces. Their only relief is when they finish their workout and lower their arms, shoulders, and chests and exclaim, "Whew!" What we speculate is that if this stresswalking is continued, the body attitude will tend to become chronic and habitual. These walkers are building up their muscles and carriage to maintain that posture on an almost permanent basis.

Start by bending your arms at a right angle at the elbow. Note what happens to your rhythm. Note what happens to your shoulders. Did your shoulders begin to hunch up? Do you feel tense? Did you feel awkward? Most people we have worked with over the years report these feelings with their arms bent that high even for a slow speed.

Relax your arms. Now, as you increase your speed, bend the elbow in even, gradual increments to match your speed. Be sensitive to the body's wanting to make the adjustment naturally. The elbow should be held firm but not locked or rigid. The arm should be swung as one unit. That means it should not be flailing about. The arm swing is in counterbalance to your leg and hip swing. Each arm swings in synch with the leg on the other side of the body.

Arm Swing Emphasis on the Backswing

The emphasis of the arm swing should be on the backswing, not the forward swing. There are valid reasons for this. The backswing of the arm works to align

71

the spine squarely over the legs. The backswing creates the proper countertorque for the hips to rotate forward.

The backswing allows the body to stay erect and provides time for the back leg to stay on the ground longer, giving you a greater push-off from your toes. It feels natural. Try it—experience the effect of the backswing of the arms for yourself. Let your body speak the truth to you. Gary Westerfield, former U.S. National Women's Race Walking coach, calls the backswing of the arms the "power position" in walking.

The power position in walking:
The emphasis on the backward arm swing allows the back leg to be extended behind the body and stay on the ground a fraction longer, giving you a greater push-off through to the toes.

WHAT TO DO WITH THOSE ARMS

Don't flail your arms all over the place. To get the right angle for swinging your arms, imagine you are standing at the center of a huge clockface, facing 12 o'clock. Your right arm should swing forward toward 12 o'clock and backward toward 5 o'clock. Your left arm should swing forward toward 12 o'clock and backward toward 7 o'clock.

As for the hands, keep them softly closed as if you were carrying a delicate object of your choice. The hands should be in line with the arm.

Making a tight fist creates tension in the arms and that tension is transmitted to the rest of the body. Make a fist only if you are expecting some danger from another walker with tight fists, a grimacing face, hunched shoulders and bad posture coming toward you pumping his arms like a prizefighter.

CHAPTER 6

Walking from Your Center

Throughout history many disciplines and movement techniques advocated the importance of the "center." The Chinese teach us that the center of our being is located directly below the belly button. The practice of yoga encourages movement from the core or center. Tai chi achieves core mobility by asking its participants to perform the movements in slow motion.

The Center of Movement in Walking

For any of us to walk with a proper gait and balance requires that we initiate walking motion from the body's *center of movement*. This center of movement, in our experience, is located about two inches above your belly button. When we initiate movement from this center, our posture and our spine will be aligned. The movement of the body will be smooth, natural, elegant, and least stressful. However, if this center of movement has been shifted to another part of the body, the movement can be awkward, strained, tense, and "uncentered." For example, walking styles that suggest vigorous swinging of the arms can shift this center to a higher position toward the upper back, leading to hunched shoulders and strained, awkward movements.

In walking, dancing, or any activity that involves the legs, the average person tends to lift the leg from the hip joint to initiate the motion. This shifts the center of movement to near the hip joint. In muscular language, you flex the leg by shortening the rectus femoris muscle. In plain language, this way of moving is indoctrinated into us from early childhood by that often heard expression, "Pick up your feet" or "Pick up your leg," and so we do.

The inevitable result is that lifting the leg and knee is the primary movement style in walking for many people in our time. When that person "picks up" his leg and knee, whether it is done consciously or not, he must hold the hip or pelvis in a rigid manner in order to be able to lift the weight of the leg and take a step forward. This style of walking is a very different movement from the job that nature designed the legs to do. The lifting of the legs is the beginning of the poor posture that is inherent in the walking styles of many middle-aged and elderly people.

Natural, balanced walking calls for the progression of the leg and knee to move straight forward and straight back—not just forward and not by lifting the leg from the hip. To do it correctly, you need to move from the core of the body, from the center of it.

Nature is wondrous in its design of the human body. Some of our body parts are visible, some are imbedded deep at our core level. Strong, balanced, rhythmic walking starts from one of these body parts imbedded deep in our core—the psoas muscles (also called the illio-psoas).

The Filet Mignon of Muscles

One of the more lucid and informed accounts of the role and biomechanics of the psoas is found in Ida Rolf's book *Rolfing: The Integration of Human Structure*. She notes that you can move beautifully with the equipment that nature has willingly provided you with, if you give it a try. Your goal is to walk with a smooth gliding stride, not a jerky pogo-stick action of lifting the legs without as much as a twitch in the hips—as if the legs were springs attached at the hip. They're not—they're attached not at the hip, but further up, above the hips. Once you realize this—by walking from your center—there will be a greater sense of relaxation to your walk, a sense of elegance, an easier swing of your hip backward and forward. You will gain a far greater support from your neglected backbone, which will produce a naturally magnificent posture. Once you've seen yourself in action, and then try to go back to the old way, you will see that lifting the legs makes you look older, more tired, and awkward.

When you initiate your walk from your center, you

will feel more secure, balanced, and have a greater sense of power to your walk. Most of this effect is courtesy of the psoas, the filet mignon of muscle in the cow and a quality muscle in the human, too.

The psoas muscles, major and minor, are perhaps the most important of all the muscles in the body in determining human upright posture and in shaping movement. The psoas muscles play a vital role not only in walking and running but also in the sexual act. Yes, learning to walk from the core will also improve your sex life. The psoas is a major part of the musculature that moves the pelvic girdle back and forth during the sex act. When the psoas is tight, the motion of the sex act is hard to accomplish and you get tired easily. When you walk from the psoas, the body core is allowed to be relaxed and energetic. So as your walking improves, so can your sex life.

Walking from the center starts with the leg flexing through the activation of the psoas muscle, not through lifting of the leg. It involves the body at its core level. Even though the "average" person seems to experience their leg flexing starting at the hip joint, it really starts much higher than that. Each step is initiated at a point just below your shoulder blades in the front of your backbone. Again, this motion does not start in the legs; the legs move in response to the action in and above the hips. This is the critical point: The leg movement is initiated in the trunk of the body and then transmitted to the legs through the flexing of the psoas muscle. In other words the legs do not originate the motion, but rather support the body and follow the initial action in the psoas.

Now we all know that the leg bone connects to the

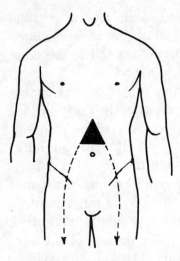

Center of Movement in Walking: This center of movement in walking is located about two inches above your belly button. When you initiate your walking motion from this center, your posture and your spine will come into alignment. The motion of the body will be fluid, natural, centered, and elegant.

pelvis and hip. But we also now know that the leg does not end at the hip both structurally and functionally. Your legs extend to the bottom of your ribs via the psoas muscle. Because the psoas forms a bridge between the legs and the upper body, its tone, vitality, and use affects many functions of the body. Breathing,

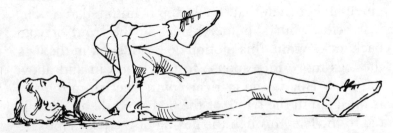

Stretching your psoas:
With your body relaxed on the floor, gently pull one leg at a time toward your chest, then both legs together. Hold a comfortable stretch for twenty-five seconds. Repeat each stretch about three times. Make sure to keep your lower back flat against the floor. Excellent stretch for your back, legs, and psoas.

digestion, elimination, and reproduction, and all basic locomotion functions are affected by the well-being of this muscle. This muscle being balanced and stretched pays big dividends on many accounts. The wavelike, undulating, rhythmic motion starts with this muscle.

So again, to visualize and to feel the leg motion starting from your center is something you need to practice and do at all times. Just think, or really just feel—your legs just grew by about a foot. The legs got longer.

When you start your walk, imagine your legs beginning a few inches above the belly button and closer to your spine. Your legs will seem longer, your movement smoother. You will start to develop a gliding action—not a lifting action—of the leg. Keep practicing this motion. It may feel unfamiliar at first but the pay-off is quite substantial once it is learned. This gentle undulating motion will serve you well as it massages your body into its full relaxed and alive potential. The power that is released from this gentle massage is unique to every walker.

It has been described as a feeling of oneness, as a feeling of universal joy, as a feeling of connectedness with the earth. There are others who felt awkward in the initial phases of learning (as with Evelyn in Chapter Two) but given time have acquired mastery and much benefit from their patience and perseverance.

CHAPTER 7

Slower Is Better

In the beginning, slower is better.

One of the hardest jobs in coaching proper walking technique is to slow down the walker's speed so that he can feel the distinct sensations of the movement. Protest, mild revolt, discomfort, and rebellion are the usual responses. The walker will express concern that he or she will not reach the target heart rate, will not get an aerobic benefit. Sometimes we'll hear the complaint that people are passing them by on the road because they are not fast enough.

Patiently we explain that slower is better in the beginning and that the added attention to detail and consciousness will pay high dividends. The analogy to this is viewing a videotape in slow motion. A great deal of detail can be observed from that slower process. The initial sense of balance can be achieved only through the experience of that process.

Stride Length and Overstriding

Overstriding, or taking long steps, is disruptive to your rhythm, is not very attractive to your walking style, and is ultimately tiring in the long run. Strive to make your steps shorter. This will automatically slow you down, which is good, at first. Later on, when you've learned balanced and centered walking, you can quicken your pace. Taking overly long steps makes your body bob up and down. It becomes mechanical walking devoid of any fluidity and rhythm.

Shorter steps allow your hips to get a good workout, and are far more balancing for your body. They will give you that sense of fluidity and rhythm that your body is ultimately seeking. Using your hips to get that

Two examples of overstriding:
A. *Walker overstriding with arched back.*
B. *Walker leaning forward taking overly long strides.*

81

added stride length will tone, strengthen, and give you the power to move great distances.

Try short fast steps, try long steps—feel the difference. Feel what happens to your rhythm and your body.

The Feet

It has been said that balance in the body begins with the feet. Humans are upright beings being increasingly pulled by gravity toward the center of the earth. Gravity pulls us down to the earth; our bones keep us from collapsing into a formless mass.

A balanced body allows us to feel more secure in the earth's gravitational field, and by living in harmony with gravity we can relax and stop bracing against it. Balance leads to relaxation. A balanced body leads to a balanced mind. The more you touch and feel the ground under you, the more the ground will touch and support you. Sounds poetic, does it not? It's also Isaac Newton's third law of physics (for every action there is an equal and opposite reaction). He made great poetry out of pure physics. The making contact and feeling the contact between the feet and the earth represents the individual's contact with the basic realities of his existence. We are all rooted in the earth and identified in our bodies.

In a very broad sense our feeling the earth, our grounding—if we may use the word—helps us more fully identify with our basic animal nature. Our lower-half of the body is where we have a fine sensory capacity of our animal nature, the power in our lower spine, our pelvic muscles, our locomotion, our sexuality, our elimination. It is here where the qualities of rhythm and grace reside, where our more instinctive nature lies.

Our feet let us know where we stand. Any tension or stiffness in our limbs reduces the sensitivity to feeling the earth. This loss of contact, this loss of balance has flooded our vernacular with phrases such as "I can't stand it," "the person has no standing," "he can't take a stand," "he's standoffish."

The well-balanced person is balanced well on his feet. He is "rooted," she is "standing for" something. Being grounded is being in reality, having our feet on the ground, being in the here and now, and taking responsibility for our lives. She is stable, he stands on firm ground. On the physical level, being "well-balanced" and grounded is indicated by openness of breathing and awareness and lack of emotional blocks. It's important

Open and relaxed feet:
Open and relax your feet as you walk.

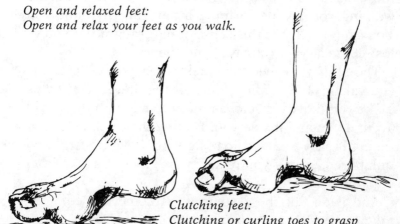

Clutching feet:
Clutching or curling toes to grasp
the earth as you walk can lead
to pain and muscle tension and rigidity.

not to curl or clutch your toes to the ground as you walk, keep them open and relaxed.

That's a lot to lay on the feet, but they are made by nature and time to withstand much weight and miles of responsibility. They can also give us much support and much pleasure.

Reach Out and Touch the Earth

Taking it easy at first will allow you to feel the earth with your feet. This may sound silly, but feeling the earth is an important element of rhythmic walking. Walking is quite different from the other forms of exercise, in that we never lose contact with the ground. Running and jogging involve a series of springlike hops and we lose contact with the ground during each hop.

If your walking is going to help you feel more secure, stress-free, and liberated, it's vital for you to feel that the earth is supporting you, and that when you are walking you are performing a natural, rhythmic act. You cannot achieve this sense of natural grace if you've lost contact with your feet and the earth.

The ability to feel the earth when you walk is the equivalent of "stopping to smell the flowers." It helps make you more conscious and in touch with the world around you and inside you. Feeling the earth is part of taking it easy—part of making your walk graceful and unlabored, even if you're steaming along at a race-level clip.

And if any of these steps don't come immediately, take our advice and don't try harder, try softer. All of us humans seem to use excessive effort in practically anything that we engage in. We anticipate that we need more effort than is actually needed and so tend to brace ourselves for a tougher task than the one at hand.

In exaggerated fitness walking, as in almost everything else, we use more energy, more force, more tension, more calories than is required. Self-conscious persons made more self-conscious by unnatural ways to move show this in tenser bodies and ever more awkward styles of movement. Exercise programs with mechanically repeated movements can undoubtedly add strength and stamina to our bodies, but they do little to correct body image or our faulty mechanisms of moving. They can actually increase postural defects.

It is unfortunate that so much in our culture seems to equate intensity with pleasure. The psychophysical pioneers F.M. Alexander and M. Feldenkrais both were quite adamant in their views that tension leads to contraction and contraction of our bodies is a process that leads to premature aging, lack of suppleness, and a physically limited life-style. "Uptight," "bent out of shape," "wired," "tight as a drum" are phrases in our vocabulary that point out these physical states.

Take Time to Visualize

In sports and in some therapeutic techniques which use mirroring or physical empathy to achieve a sense of the performance of the activity, you can get a kinesthetic response in which your body feels the sense of the movement. The idea here is to convert this visual information into motor memory, in other words, to make any visualization tangible.

It is effective on many levels to do this form of learning. But it is important to choose a model who is highly skilled and coordinated at what you are attempting to learn. Copycatting someone who walks badly can be a real drag on your body language and image. Modeling yourself after a rhythmic, graceful person can be a wonderful union of human experiences. So be a prudent shopper for a model that feels and looks good to your body.

During some part of your walk focus your attention on yourself. Imagine yourself walking with style—confident, free-flowing, strong, healthy. To the best of your ability create an image of yourself, even if you do not "see" yourself in your mind's eye. Just by concentrating on that mental image, your mind will absorb the knowledge anyway. You can practice this visualization even for a few seconds anytime, anywhere during the day.

Breathing

At times we actually have to remind some of the people in our walking classes to breathe. It seems to be a common practice for many people to actually hold their breath when they are learning new ways to move or even think.

Breathing can be a problem for some people who for years have blocked out feelings with shallow breathing and a tightly contracted belly dating back to their infancy. Fears, disappointments, pains, all those many hurts that were cut off from expression by holding the breath and cutting off feelings. In motion and sustained motion, this stranglehold of held feelings subsides because as we breathe hard in exercise and exertion, it's harder to hold on to all those feelings. This is especially true in relaxed deep breathing. As the breath flows in, some of those contained emotions flow out. Be aware of the fact that some of the discomfiture felt in deep breathing could be the unacknowledged feelings held for long periods of time.

We should state that once some of these feelings are expressed and felt, the tightness and tension holding them begin to ease their grip. It can be emotionally cleansing. Keep in mind that breathing more deeply can tap that reservoir of joy and pleasure and ecstasy, so there are many and varied experiences we mortals are heir to. So breathe on, fellow mortal.

Breathing Better at Faster Speeds

In his book *The Breathplay Approach to Wholelife Fitness*, Ian Jackson gives some excellent advice concerning the connection between breath and motion. Jackson's approach teaches breath and body awareness and emphasizes how controlled exhalation stretches the spine for improved posture and good rhythm. The main point of his breathing work focuses on an active outbreath (exhalation) using abdominal and thoracic muscles to squeeze air from the lungs and create a partial vacuum to facilitate a passive inhalation.

Actively forcing air from the lungs flattens the stomach, lifts pelvic bone as it tucks the tail bone and ultimately flattens the lower-back area. The traditional "belly breathing" with its active inhalation and resultant stomach distension is not recommended in activities involving upright posture because it increases the lower-back curve and tends to be fatiguing. We have also found that with "belly breathing" when we walk tends to cause people to hold their breath for a moment after the belly is "full of air." The breathing is less rhythmic that way.

So we do recommend active exhalation and passive inhalation. It requires some practice and concentration to master but it will definitely improve your oxygen uptake and give you more energy and life as you learn it.

Stretching Our Bodies

Because of lack of time, lack of caring, few of us stretch our bodies anymore. Our chronically contracted state is seen as practically normal. But it is not. Animals stretch all the time. It's not even a habit; it's inherent in their nature. Are we that removed from our animal nature that we have forgotten one of nature's greatest rebalancers: stretching?

Our walking approach will bring a bit of a stretch to your normal everyday walking. You don't have to take up any extra time to do it. You can do it as part of your walk. As part of your life. No waste, no time out. Each and every walking step can revive your body's needs for movement and the delicious freedom that comes from a good stretch. When you add that extra movement to your hips you are, in effect, generating more flexibility to the entire hip socket and also loosening the lower back.

As you step out with your legs from your walking center, you will be adding to the flexibility of your entire torso, and as you develop a smoother arm swing, your shoulder socket will be freed from some of the tightness that comes from contraction. By developing more rhythm in your walk, you will be unknotting kinks and muscle tensions and providing your body with that wonderful feeling that comes from increased flexibility. As your posture improves, your spine will stay alive instead of sinking into the tightness of gravity that causes compression of the vertebrae through the aging process. The more you are walking correctly, the more you maintain the openness that comes from an unrestricted stretchlike motion.

How Much Should You Walk?

Why have you forgotten about yourself? Why have you compartmentalized your life into work, home, exercise, family, friends, self-improvement—all seen and experienced as separate items on a menu? Remember, each of those morsels can make up a satisfying meal. So walking can be the great "meal" your body will love and needs, too. Now, viewed from this perspective let us ask: How much should you walk? Our answer: As much as possible. We encourage people to use their walking as "transportation" to and from work, if feasible. We support "walk" breaks instead of "coffee" breaks—or walking instead of lunching. We also recommend backpacks for these walk-to-work walks, leaving hands free to participate in a brisk, alive stride.

The basic idea is to help you discover practical times to walk, incorporating the activity into the flow of your life and not as an extra task.

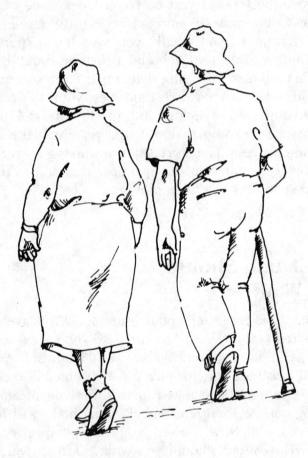

Awareness Is the Key

The essence of our teaching method is that you will learn to walk well at any speed. The acquisition of a dancelike rhythmic vibrant walk is imprinted in our genes. By focusing awareness on our most natural motion, you can release that which is due you and waiting to come out. The work is in acquiring that awareness. It is not the quantity of miles you put in but the quantity of minutes that you pay attention to awareness. Awareness is the key. Awareness is being in the moment. Awareness is paying attention to what is happening right now. Awareness is being involved in the process of the doing—and not in the final goal.

Learning how to walk faster will be easy once you have learned how to slow down. Give yourself the rewards for paying attention to the moment, for being aware of your motion. Giving yourself rewards for the miles you walk can be a secondary reward.

Be aware first. Now, in that willingness to be aware will come the recognition of the twinges, discomforts, awkwardness, uneasiness, possible embarrassment, self-consciousness, vanity, frustration, and the host of disruptive, downside emotions that accompany learning anything new. And how you grow through these moments of disorientation into accomplishment can signal increased awareness—because instead of rushing through your discomforts you will become conscious of them. Instead of avoiding uneasiness you will learn to pass through it with your senses alert and participating. This is the skill of mastery brought to the simple human function of walking. And because this skill is being developed around such a normal, natural

91

function you will be able to participate in the greatest healing force in the world—awareness and consciousness in action.

In our classes, workshops, and individual sessions we constantly refer to our walking method as a loving action. Every move is built on what we do naturally and the gradual expansion of those moves to encompass a greater range of motion and possibility. It is a loving approach to the body.

CHAPTER 8

Rhythm and Posture—
Poetry in Motion!

Consider for a moment the famous walk of Marilyn Monroe, or the distinctive swagger of John Wayne. Here were two celebrities whose distinctive hip motion made their walking style memorable. Now we're not suggesting that you imitate theirs or anyone else's style. We are encouraging you to loosen up a bit. No, you don't have to waddle or wiggle, or sashay or sway. No exaggeration is necessary. Nothing unnatural in this balanced and centered walk. Just a touch of dance, a hint of your own natural rhythm expressed easily and comfortably. Maybe you can be known for your walk, too.

Even better, you can find the poetic movement that is inside of us all. The secret is to just find your point of relaxation and freedom, the place where your body glides, floats, and lets out a deep sigh of relief. We're sure that you have enjoyed the pleasure of dancing at some time in your life. Well, that's the pleasurable sensation we want you to go for in your walk. Whether you boogie to the sounds of rock 'n' roll, lilt to a waltz, brighten to folk dancing, bounce to the vibrations of aerobic dance classes, or groove on the Brazilian samba—somewhere in your body is the instinct to dance. So let yourself begin to think of your walks as the dance of walking. Every one of you can find a bounce and spring in your step. There's no need to lunge, stride, or push yourself to gain those exercise benefits you want. We're not just going for aerobic points—we're after poetry in motion.

Three Dimensions of Movement

In the first dimension of movement, we sway forward and back. The second-dimension movement is from one side to the other, keeping centered over the weight-bearing foot. In the third dimension our body moves up and down with each step as the foot supports us with the "impact" on the earth. What this means is that, ideally, the body moves in a rhythmic, graceful, dancelike motion and *not in a mechanical, robotically perfect straight line.* When you swing your arm back and forth as you walk, it does not swing back and forth in a straight line. It actually swings back and forth in a narrow figure-eight motion. This important principle, called counterbalance, establishes equilibrium in motion. In walking you can feel the upper and lower body parts moving and shifting in opposing directions to maintain balance. As your arm moves forward, the opposite leg will move back. This counterbalancing can be seen in all three dimensions of movement. As we walk, the body balances itself from side to side, forward and backward, up and down, and diagonally.

The dictionary definition of undulation reads "to move in a smooth wavelike motion" or "a regular rising and falling of movement to alternating sides. Movement in waves." The feeling of walking well can be as smooth as the glide of a dolphin cutting its way through water. The undulating wavelike motions that your body is making cut through the air and space and your body is literally swimming forward. It also can be described as riding the crests and ebbs of a gentle wave in the ocean. Your body balancing itself effortlessly with every motion and wave. Feel that, and it will be hard for you to go back to the shore again.

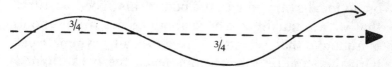

The Undulating Motion of Your Body:
When we walk, we move our bodies in a wavy undulating
fashion. We do not walk the straight and narrow but actually
move about ¾ of an inch to the left and right and up and down
from the direction of travel. Nearly all motion in the body should
be fluid, circular, and rotating and in that way involves more
muscles.

This requires remarkable coordination and rhythm. Babies learn this rhythm. But as we make the transition from babyhood to childhood to adolescence to adulthood, most of us lose our sense of that rhythm. It's sort of like having the poetry in us edited into a rigid set of signs: Bend those arms! Keep those hips still!

And instead of a true sense of balance, we end up with small distortions, little crookednesses here and there, with our circulation impaired, joints and bones bearing added stresses. Our body just starts to bend and stretch in unhealthy ways. With added tensions in our muscles, we begin to feel out of sorts, uptight, uncomfortable, lacking in energy, and wondering what doctor to call.

Posture Is Not Static

Posture is not standing or sitting rigidly, straight as a board. It's dynamic—constantly moving and adjusting the body to maintain good balance. Most of our ideas and notions of proper posture and alignment are based on an ideal symmetry in the body. This "good posture" that we are taught and hear about comes from schools of thought that see the body as ideally symmetrical, with the shoulders level, hips level, the back aligned, and a straight vertical alignment of your body from the top of your head, through your body's center, to the bottom of your feet.

But it is only "at attention" that we begin to look somewhat symmetrical. From what we know of human movement, we move in an asymmetrical, three-dimensional, wavelike, undulating motion. We do not walk like straight sticks.

RHYTHM AND POSTURE—POETRY IN MOTION!

You're in the Army Now!

"HA-TENSION!!" barks the sergeant and the recruits scamper into position:

Chest thrust out . . .
Chin in . . .
Shoulders back . . .
Stomach in . . .
Pelvis tucked under . . .
Legs straight . . .

In many of the instructions given new recruits into the walking-for-fitness world—the military posture seems to be a favorite. The posture does, for some, indicate authority, confidence, strength, and power. But it can also represent rigidity, poor posture, shallow breathing, and a false, masked front. It is also hard to walk rhythmically when you are at HA-TENSION. You are literally "AT TENSION."

In his book *Narcissism—The Denial of the True Self,* Alexander Lowen, M.D., makes the point that "inhibiting movement through chronic muscular tension has the effect of suppressing feeling. Such tension produces a rigidity in the body, a partial deadness. It is not surprising that soldiers are drilled in standing at attention. As we have seen, a good soldier must suppress much feeling and become, in effect, a killing machine."

Marching can be the most aggressive form of walking and when it is performed with a stiff-legged kicking action, the goose-step, it has been used by governments to intimidate civilians over the ages.

The Ramrod Posture Theory

Walking gracefully and effortlessly with a minimum of strain is what feels good and has the most healing effect on the body. But not so in the French Foreign Legion, where the proverbial ramrod theory of walking posture was the rule, states Gerald Donaldson, in his wonderful book called *The Walking Book*. Here the erect ramrod posture was the order of the day and to achieve this end, writes Donaldson, "a coin was placed between the buttocks of a raw recruit and he was ordered to march around without dropping the money."

Incidentally, some other walking instructors have suggested using walnuts instead of the coins. We advocate a natural, coin free, nut free way to better health and happiness through walking well.

March to a Different Drummer

While we are talking about the army, what about marching music, which we know a lot of people love to listen to when they walk? David loves to walk with John Philip Sousa marches playing in his Walkman. It is a very exhilarating feeling for him to walk down the street or in the park to the steady beat of the drums and the bugle. But he modifies his walking to marching music quite extensively. He drops his shoulders, relaxes his chest, lets his belly and chin relax, and gets his hips doing the motion to the beat of the drum. Fantastic feeling. He could conquer any terrain with the power achieved by relaxing into the natural motion of the body.

The important fact here is that the walking motion is initiated from that center, that ever widening center just below the sternum in the chest. When you walk or march from there, many of the characteristics of good posture fall right into place. You will achieve that power and strength, yet be relaxed and vibrant at the same time. Your pelvis will align and your shoulders drop down, yet your abdominal muscles will allow you to breathe fully.

So don't give up your marching by any means. Just modify it to be a little kinder to your body. This way you can breathe, have some feelings, feel a great deal of power and still strut around with rhythm and fluidity.

So AT-EASE recruits. And strike up the band.

To Lean or Not to Lean

So much has been written about proper posture, alignment, standing straight, and gravity. You get the advice from articles and some walking advocates that you should lean a few degrees, usually about five degrees, into the direction of the travel, to achieve a faster walk. Nobody quite explains why or how it will make you go faster. Nor is there proper advice as to when the lean should take place or if it should take place at all. This advice to lean should only be given on a case by case basis by somebody trained to observe gait and biomechanics of the moving body. There is a point at push-off from the back leg when the body will lean forward and the center of gravity falls in anticipation of the next heel-strike.

The body leans all by itself and we are careful not to give this unnecessary instruction to everyone. It can be damaging to your back and can lead to injuries and lower-back problems. When the body is off-balance it exacts a great effort to right itself. You spend energy and tension to keep yourself from falling and the body posture is miserable. You probably feel miserable, too, once you become aware of this added bodily stress.

Many walkers tend to lean backward a few degrees, some forward a few degrees. Some lean to the right and some lean to the left. Most of these walkers are not aware that they lean. In our work or in the clinics, we will pull aside the people with significant leans and have them experience what it feels like to actually stand straight. They stand relaxed, with head, shoulders, torso, pelvis, and legs aligned and straight, and they are amazed by the sensation.

The walkers that lean backward now feel that they are going to fall over forward. We have them stay in that position a few minutes with constant adjustments as they will tend to revert back to their old tilt. We ask them to try and set to memory what a proper vertical alignment feels like. We have them breathe into the posture for a few moments, let them relax into it.

It's important to *experience* corrected posture, not just think about it. During a coached walk, constant reminders are given to walkers to maintain alignment. It's easy to revert within seconds to the old habit, what "feels normal." Walkers need to be reminded over and over until the new walking pattern takes hold. Until body and mind establish a motor memory of the pattern and it becomes automatic, constant attention and awareness needs to be heightened to offset the years of neglect.

The purpose of our approach is to help you learn to allow that coordinated series of movements to flow freely and give you a full range of dynamic balance and posture. Our aim is to restore your body to a natural muscular symmetry which is relatively free of habitual stresses and pent-up tensions. You will walk around speaking of your diminished burdens, your new sense of lightness, and the effortless way in which you now move. You will express poetry in motion every time you take a step.

Help for the Overweight
and Underwalked

It's been said and said again—IN ORDER TO BOTH LOSE
EXTRA WEIGHT AND TO MAINTAIN A WHOLESOME WEIGHT YOU
HAVE TO MOVE MORE THAN YOU ARE MOVING!

And walking is simply the best possible movement
around because that's what you do naturally. But
you're probably not doing it enough or with enough
rhythmic energy to have any real effect.

All the warnings in the world can't help you. All the
hype about the best diet in the world or the easiest
weight-loss method won't magically melt down those
excess pounds. But walking with that extra bit of
awareness for that extra minute for that extra block
will build into a real and sustainable physical activity
that will be there for all your life.

It's very, very hard to shift from that couch-potato
life-style. We know that and we won't promise you an

easy answer, but we do know that *you can do it.* Start moving slowly and gradually, when you are ready, when you have made an inner decision to undo some of the damage that a sedentary life-style produces.

We know, too, that if your excess weight tips over fifty pounds that your struggle is painful and difficult. But we know that you can still undo the damage, physical and emotional, that comes from wearing a body that is too big for your needs. Just knowing that a simple, twenty-minute a day walk will start up your sluggish metabolism and get your body to start burning its fuel—food—more efficiently could be enough encouragement to get you started. We can also promise you your appetite will drop.

If you're a thin couch-potato whose bones are getting a little softer each day, then that same simple twenty minutes a day will keep your bones stronger and more solid. For those who suffer from overweight, who feel the real painful physical effects of too many pounds, those first few steps of walking can be painful.

One of our clients told us how she used to feel her body "jiggle" as soon as she moved it and that made her only hate herself even more. Since one of us would go walking with her, she had an opportunity to share her deep feelings of hurt and anger. "But what would I do without you?" she sobbed one day during her walking session. "I could never go through this alone. My body just feels so awkward to me ... bouncing around and I get out-of-breath so easily."

Because of her desperation, we formed small groups of walkers who were thirty or more pounds overweight. We encouraged the walkers to join together and learn how to help each other during the hardship of getting started. We met with the group for only six weeks—enough time to get some momentum going—and then sent them on their way. Most of the group stayed together and they checked in with us from time to time for support and encouragement. By the end of the year, everyone had lost at least twenty pounds and was feeling optimistic and satisfied. We had advised everyone to be realistic about their goals—to get moving first and then to learn to adjust their eating habits. Trying to do both would result in conflicts and crisis. Our little experimental group hung in there, and gradually everyone created personally satisfying health habits.

We also advise you to find a buddy to start off your self-renewal journey. Or at least let someone who cares for you know that you are embarking on an exciting and scary journey. Let them know you just need to talk from time to time and that you don't expect them to do anything for you—even if what you want is a pat on the back. This simple exercise in communication will help you stay with your second baby steps out into the world.

Remember, you already went through baby steps when you started to toddle around in early childhood. And even if you fell into bad eating and activity habits as early as adolescence or even before, you can still try stepping out again. This time, though, your baby steps can walk you away from the refrigerator or that cozy couch and take you to a more joyous life.

Joanne, at forty-two, looked like she had fought a long and losing battle with the bulge. She seemed to be carrying an extra forty pounds on her body and had a slumped, self-conscious air about her. She was somewhat shy and told us that she worked in middle management in a small corporation. She also told us about her interest in learning how to live a healthier, more positive life-style. It seems that both her parents suffered from heart problems and Joanne genuinely wanted to take solid, reliable, preventative steps to ensure her own health.

She confessed that she was not particularly athletic and never even enjoyed athletics, but she knew she had to do something. And sooner, not later. She talked about how she had kept putting off and putting off taking some action; and she told us about how she would start on a diet and exercise program, stay on it for a while and then . . . kaput. She was feeling frustrated and angry at herself for her undisciplined habits. "I can't even begin to tell you how many diets I've tried," Joanne said sadly. She sighed heavily and her body slumped even more into the chair. "I've even tried hypnosis and biofeedback and meditation techniques. Any time I read or hear of anything that sounds worthwhile I give it a try. But then I lose interest. I get so angry with myself and continue eating."

"And then you really can't do anything, isn't that true?" Deena asked. This was a familiar refrain we had heard many, many times. But each time, with each person, we felt the distress of that individual person. We understand. Everyone thinks they're supposed to be some kind of superhero accomplishing tremendous feats of control and discipline. And even though we all know that that's impossible, we look around us and think "Well, that person seems to have their life so in control. What's wrong with me?" Deena said.

"The fact is we're all human beings and vulnerable and imperfect and foolish and inconsistent and we don't seem to want to admit that," David added. She responded that she had to deal with that "fact" all the time and she was always feeling stressed at her job, where the pressure to be perfect or to be in control just ate at her. "And then I start to overeat," she lamented. "It feels like the puppy chasing its tail again and again. I just go around and around the same circle, and I never get anywhere. Sometimes it feels like I can't even catch my breath during the day. And what's even more frustrating is that I know there is something I can do that will work for me; I just haven't hit on it yet."

"Are you concerned about how you appear to others?" Deena asked.

"Of course I'm concerned," she answered curtly. "Appearance counts for a lot these days." There was despair in Joanne's voice, the old self put-down again. Sometimes we think a major part of our work is just guiding people through the muddy waters of low self-esteem. First, by helping them hear they way they put themselves down and then by guiding, teaching and coaching them to come out of this hurtful image of themselves so that they feel good about themselves, both physically and mentally. That's a cornerstone of real inner and outer health and it's one of our guiding principals. So the first step is always to admit your insecurity and not to cover it over.

Joanne seemed really encased in her body, like that layer of fat was a cushion for her against the world. When she started walking on the treadmill she was filled with apology for her awkwardness, her clumsiness. Her shoulders were slumped and she tended to keep her head down, almost shamefaced about her appearance. Joanne had a really pretty face and even with her overweight, there was a grace and lightness about her movements that were inconsistent with her comments about her ungainliness. A tall, large-boned woman with ample hips, Joanne was the picture of self-consciousness.

And when David showed her how to walk that imaginary line and her hips started moving more freely, Joanne froze. "I've got to stop," she insisted. David stopped the treadmill and Joanne seemed shaken. She looked at him so earnestly and with such hurt that he realized some raw nerve had been touched. All of a sudden Joanne was spilling out a story, a personal story of pain and confusion.

Joanne talked plaintively about how she had been in a battle with her body since early childhood. Her mother had stopped touching her when Joanne was five years old and was always critical of Joanne's appearance, her walk, her body. And by the time Joanne reached adolescence, her height only added to her burden of feeling unworthy. She adopted the slumping posture of children who are tall for their age, plus she told us of feeling horribly self-conscious about developing breasts. "I guess I pushed it far away from my thoughts. It all became part of me. But when David started telling me to open up my chest and to move my hips, all of a sudden I was hit by this memory."

Over the next six sessions Joanne came to talk, to walk, to learn. And each time she tried another step the fear was there right with her. But she kept on walking taller, walking stronger, walking with her head lifted. And she kept on opening up even while she reported on her fears. Only now instead of letting her fears stop her she was facing them, slowly, step by step.

"This is so simple, so natural," she would comment at moments when she allowed her body to take over. And then she would contract, get tense, feel frightened and want to stop. Much of her first two hours were spent stopping and moving and stopping and moving. Again, with our encouragement she was able to get through the rough ride of her fears and inner demons.

By the third session Joanne was beginning to develop a more powerful sense of herself and her walk showed it. She was beginning to thaw out. She noticed that the low-grade chronic lower-back pain with which she lived was beginning to ease. She was beginning to recognize that she had a choice between walking more openly and feeling better, or tightening up again and having the ache recur.

We continued to hear from Joanne as she embarked on her new program of walking for life. Instead of referring to it as "exercise," she simply began to allow more time for walking so that it became second nature.

Indeed, to walk for life is not really a program. It's more a wholesome relationship with yourself. Like too many people, Joanne was eager to discover a "program" or a "routine" that would bring her the joys of good health, inner and outer. Yet, try as she did, with each new "program" or diet or gimmick, she would eventually lose interest because it wasn't built on her needs. Though she had access to the tremendous resources of corporate fitness centers or health clubs, she still couldn't find something that would hold her interest. But she yearned for the positive life-style and found unexpected treasures in this simple approach. And for Joanne especially, just understanding the story her body was telling allowed her to learn to walk more openly and to become more trusting of herself. After getting into the "walking habit" Joanne began to pay closer attention to both her diet and her eating patterns. And by that time she was also feeling much better about herself since her body was no longer her enemy. Now she approached her body more as a stranger she was interested in befriending. And it worked. It took Joanne a full year to turn around her negative self-image and her careless eating habits. Even today, Joanne tells us, that she realizes it will take more years of steady effort to establish a solid foundation of secure eating . . . but as for her walking, why Joanne says she wouldn't miss that for even one day!

The journey of a thousand miles begins with one step. Remember this ancient wisdom. It has traveled over the centuries to remind you that you too can begin the long journey to enjoyable health with just one walking step.

CHAPTER 10

High-Tech Walking and High-Tech Visualization

On those lazy, hazy days of summer or those icy snowy days of winter, or nights for all that matter—any time of year and any time of day—a treadmill in the home is very handy.

So many uses come to mind. You don't have to put on makeup or fix your hair or wear your best pair of leotards or T-shirt. In fact, you can literally walk naked on a treadmill with the precaution that a pair of shoes do come in handy to protect you from that rubberized moving surface.

Just think, you don't need to drive to the track, call a friend to join you, worry about muggers and dogs or bees or mosquitoes. There are no bicycles or cars to avoid, no potholes to evade. Your own bathroom is a few steps away for pit stops. Water or juice is by your side, radio at your fingertips. TV is there to entertain you, and a phone is at hand to talk to friends. Plus, if you are on a diet and feel the need to eat something, you can hop on the treadmill for a few minutes. The increase in oxygen in your system, the exhilaration of the brief walk will appease that appetite and definitely appease your guilt. If you are tense and agitated, a few minutes of walking on that treadmill can soothe your nerves and relax you.

Sounds like paradise or someone writing an ad for treadmills, doesn't it? All of the above is true—but there are also some drawbacks to the use of the treadmill. The major one is that you miss the feeling of the great outdoors, fresh air, sun, moon, clouds, birds, traffic, other walkers, trees, nature, and civilization. If we keep in mind that the treadmill is a useful tool and not a way of life, it offers great benefits for people that can use them both at home or in gyms.

Step Up on to the Moving Belt

A treadmill is a good place to start to work on your walking stride. On the treadmill's even, secure surface, changing and adapting to different stride lengths and walking styles is an asset. The surface of the treadmill is even and very desirable because of the padded-rubber surface, the wood base and the fact that you can acutely hear the loudness of your footstep on the walking belt.

Learn to Walk
with a Softer Step

Here you can learn to walk softly and silently while feeling the surface under your feet. The principles that you learned in the "steps" section apply here as well. Walking without the heavy plodding action of the feet gives you greater mastery over your body and walking style. Walking silently and softly will reduce strain on the bottom of your feet and any shock to the rest of the system. It will also reduce the possible complaint from the neighbors downstairs wondering what that thud-thud-thud is all about in your home.

Treadmills look easy and after a little practice they are easy to walk on. But since the first few times can be challenging, start slowly. Begin by straddling the belt and starting the treadmill at the lowest speeds. Then step on and hold on to the handrails until you feel at home with the sensation of the ground moving under you. When you feel comfortable, let go of the handrail one hand at a time and take those first steps without the support of the bar. If you feel at all unsteady, grab the handrails immediately.

When you get off and the belt is still moving, always hold on to the handrail as you get off. If you talk to someone while on the treadmill, keep your eyes on the "road" as if you were driving a car and not on the person you are talking with. The belt is narrow and you do not have a lot of space to weave about.

Road and Treadmill Differences

There will be some difference between the way you walk on a treadmill and on the road. On an electric treadmill, the track is propelled along under you. On the road, you will be required to push off with your back legs to move forward. These differences add to the spice of life—see if you can note these differences for yourself. You will be asked throughout this book to learn to increase your awareness about you and your body in motion. It can be as much fun as it was to learn to walk for the first time—this new sense of self-mastery and mastery of your environment.

About Boredom

Yes, boredom is a factor. Yes, music and pacing tapes are of great help to pass the time and keep you focused on the task at foot. By all means have some *music* to help you with your rhythm and sense of fun.

As far as TV, it is our personal opinion that unless you have thoroughly mastered the treadmill and your movement on it, keep TV for your couch-potato activities. By then, you deserve to sit and watch, having done all that workout. But TV tends to be distracting and to take you away from the task at hand. Your form, your concentrations and your progress become losers by the installation of a TV in front of you. If you cannot avoid it, if you need it, do pay attention to what you are doing, at least during the commercial breaks.

Wear walking shoes while on the treadmill. The

rubber mat can be very unforgiving on bare feet. But if you decide to try it barefoot, you will learn quite soon about burning the bottom of the sole.

When you get off the treadmill you will feel a little light-headed or dizzy. Just walk around the room. This sensation will quickly pass. Most people enjoy the sensation. Do you remember turning round and round as a kid and then stopping and enjoying the sensation as the world keeps revolving? This is not quite that but fun anyhow.

The Incline

Our experience shows that the incline or hill maker on the treadmaker should be used sparingly. Most of the time in real life you will walk on level ground. Some walkers have decided to get hard workouts by setting the incline at high angles and keeping it there throughout the workout. This is not recommended. It puts strain on your back, your posture, wreaks havoc on different muscle groups and is almost the equivalent of walking on high heels for your body.

One to several degrees of incline is quite adequate to put you in the groove for a good workout. A bigger incline for a few minutes from time to time is fine but do not do it as a steady diet. Vary your experience. Be kind to your body.

Hand Weights on a Treadmill

On a treadmill is where hand weights can be used sparingly. You can see if your alignment and posture goes askew and you can always put weights down when you tire. If you are on the road, you are obligated to carry them for miles.

Mirror, Mirror on the Wall

Placing a mirror in front of the treadmill is a wonderful way of seeing yourself in action. Watching yourself and your body move reveals much to the trained and the untrained eye and with some of the tips to follow and what you have learned in the techniques section, your eye will be better trained to see your fairest and not so fair moves.

Observe Yourself in Different Walking Styles

Changing walking styles as you move and actually feeling the changes occur in your body is an amazing experience. Given some patience and practice, you can actually sense, see and feel the variety of "body statements" that emerge as you change your gait in front of the mirror. That mirror in front of you is your friend. It is you—or at least a reflection of you. You can make friends with it or it can be someone you choose to be in a struggle with. Note whether you make eye contact with yourself. Note whether you avert your eyes from certain parts of your body that you are ashamed of or disappointed with. Note the position of the shoulders, raised or relaxed; the swing of the arm; the open or closed chest; collapsed, or erect posture. Refer to Chapter Three for proper walking tips.

Some Hints to Loosen Those Hips on the Treadmill

This is an excellent exercise to increase the range of motion in the hips and waist. This exercise repeated from time to time will provide you with the sensation of how the hips can be moved in their axis. You can use this approach to open the possibilities of a looser, freer hip action. Do the following:

1. Hold on to the front handle bars with *both* hands.
2. Set the speed at 2.5 mph. Keep incline flat.
3. Imagine a line running down the center of the belt.
4. With fully erect and aligned posture, have your feet *cross* over the imaginary line. Done gently and with consciousness, this exercise will allow the hips to move with a greater range of motion and add mobility and suppleness to the hips.
5. As you cross the center line, flex your foot just a little, and that will allow your leg to straighten out further. You will feel an increased tension

in the muscles throughout the upper legs and buttocks. Do this for about two to three minutes and then revert to your regular walk.

Treadmill Buying Guide

A manual treadmill without a motor for walking is definitely not recommended. It can work for running, but not for walking. A decent electric treadmill is expensive. Trying to save money on the purchase of a treadmill may end up costing more in repairs and frustration later on. The cheap treadmills simply do not hold up in prolonged use. Shop around, talk to people who have owned one. Talk to the folks at your gym; do your research. It's an expensive item, a wonderful tool, and a great way to go nowhere for miles in the comfort of your home.

High-Tech Visualization— the Video

Camcorders, which were virtually unknown only five years ago, have become part of everyday life in much of America, and consumers are finding dozens of new uses for them. At golf courses, tennis clubs, and school gymnasiums around the country camcorders are used as training devices to videotape and play back pictures of amateur and professional athletes-in-motion. Whether you are an aspiring competitive race walker, fitness walker, everyday walker—or especially you stresswalkers—video gives you the opportunity to see and analyze how you move in space and improve on what you have.

We've all seen ourselves in still photos, but still photos can only capture a fraction of a second of the flow of human locomotion. They are but a snapshot in time. Though photos are rated to be worth a thousand words, static images are inadequate to illuminate the subtleties and dynamics of movement. Therefore we can honestly say that video is worth 10,000 pictures. Video will clearly show you how you look and reveal where you need improvement.

Videocassette players also have freeze frame and slow-motion functions which make self-analysis of your walking form, gait, and body language much easier. The videotape of your action can be played back, allowing you to make adjustments in your motion, immediately and over time.

For many walkers, the only time they have seen themselves have been in quick glimpses of their reflection in store windows or mirrors. Upon seeing yourself walking for the first time, you may find yourself saying, "I never realized I was walking that way!" So treat yourself to this wonder of modern technology and see yourself as others see you. You may think you need improvement, but you may be pleasantly surprised at the beauty and grace that you possess.

The Power of the Image

We had been teaching walking for years before we bought a camcorder for our work. We taped ourselves in different circumstances, but when we asked a friend to videotape our walking, we were quite surprised by the results. It was much more different from what we had expected. How we actually walked was very different from the mental image that we had of how we were walking. In fact, viewing ourselves objectively in motion for the first time was a startling experience. It was also a catalyst for us to improve our walking style. We were able to see what we needed to do mechanically to improve our form. Now, these ongoing videotapings of ourselves are a tool for the ongoing process of refining our biomechanics, movement patterns and body language. Our walking form made the most dramatic improvement of our walking careers during the month that followed our analysis of our first videotaping. We now tape ourselves walking on the treadmill regularly so as to continue to refine our style and balance.

Some aspects that may be interesting for you to observe are:

- That you have personal movement habits that can be analyzed;
- That your movement style is related closely to your personality;
- Your choice of sport and exercise programs emphasizes particular movement patterns;
- By emphasizing particular movement patterns, walking will tend to reinforce certain personality and habitual physical traits. These could work for you or against you depending on your emotional makeup;
- So that by knowing and understanding your movement habits, you are in a better position to select future walking programs that will help

reduce or develop specific personality and movement characteristics.

Watching yourself on video can give you useful insights into how you can improve your movement patterns. This empowers you to make decisions as to how you want to represent yourself in the world. Video can also enhance the clarity of your psychic, emotional, behavioral, and body identity. It can be a wonderful tool for self-observation and self-confrontation by analyzing your movement patterns. While past history and emotional scars are often reflected in your walking style, video provides a tool to heal and transform many of these features into a healthy positive walking motion that serves and speaks well of you.

A Woman and Her Walking Style

Here is the story of a woman in which video and a treadmill were an integral part of her growth. You get a sense of the possibilities that emerge from using videotape and a treadmill as a part of growing self-awareness.

After experiencing the benefits of our walking approach, a mother referred her twenty-seven-year-old daughter for a series of private sessions. Barbara was a lawyer in a large law office. Her research job was demanding, her hours were long and much of her work entailed hours and hours of sitting.

Barbara adamantly informed us that she was not in the least interested in "fitness" walking. She had strong opinions about how silly she thought fitness walkers looked and she wanted no part of it. She did, however, appreciate that her mother had gotten great relief through our walking approach. She had particularly noted the improvement in her mother's posture and self-confidence. That appealed to her. She even said her mother was developing a sexy walk that looked terrific.

Barbara was bothered by constant muscle tension in her neck, shoulders, lower back and upper abdomen. Her posture spoke of somebody who was constantly burdened. She admitted she felt a "heaviness" in her body, even though she had no problem with overweight. She tried to go to her gym at least twice a week where she would take an aerobics class, do some light weight training or sometimes take a yoga class. She confessed that more often than not she would just collapse into the whirlpool or take a sauna to ease her tension and fatigue.

She was aware of the toll her job was taking on her body, but she was determined and ambitious. We agreed that our function was to try to help Barbara learn how to structure walking breaks and how to use her body in such a manner that these breaks would provide maximum benefits in the short spurts she allowed herself.

Videotaped on the Treadmill

We observed Barbara walk around the office and then videotaped Barbara on the treadmill for thirty minutes at a steady, easy eighteen-minute-mile pace. When Barbara first saw her videotaped image she seemed horrified. "I look so old, so . . . so tired," she lamented. "And I feel tired a lot, it's true." Barbara's rounded shoulders looked like they were carrying the weight of the world on them, and she saw that expression very clearly on the videotape.

"I do look burdened. And I feel it too a lot of the time. But I can't just stop doing what I'm doing," Barbara complained. "I've even tried some other body techniques to help me sit better and to stand straighter. But I just fall back into my old habits. I don't see how this can help, I'll forget it as soon as I leave," she stated bitterly.

We explained that since our approach was built on walking, a new movement pattern could be assimilated in time. You can constantly be reeducating your own body with each step, we told her. Plus, she had the benefit of working with video so that she herself could chart her own improvements and not be dependent on outside commentary. Eventually she would develop a stronger, more positive feel for her body and about her body.

She voiced her frustration and her skepticism. We suggested that her tendency to frustration might be contributing to her "pain in the neck." She acknowledged that frustration was a disturbing part of her emotional life and that it affected her constantly.

But in actually seeing how her emotions affected her body, Barbara seemed motivated to learning more about herself and to try to make some concrete, practical changes. We reminded her that we were going to deal with the effects of her frustration, not the cause, and then we set about guiding Barbara to experience her body as a partner, not as the burden it had become.

First David worked on the tightness in her hips. He guided her through the moves you will learn in the clinic section of our book. Barbara was particularly tight in her lower body. It was difficult for her to sense that her hips could move with greater ease and fluidity. With the help of the sunny, lilting sounds of Brazilian samba music encouraging her, along with our support, Barbara let down her guard and eased into the sweetness of the rhythmic music. And at the same time, miracle of miracles, those uptight shoulders of hers also dropped down. We keep the music at a low sound level in our office to maintain an atmosphere of ease and support.

As that inviting rhythm made its way into Barbara's heart we could see her whole body relax. She looked at herself in the mirror in front of the treadmill and smiled at herself. Her entire body reflected the lightness and loss of tension, and she could see it, feel it and take delight in this change.

"This is so natural. Why isn't everybody learning this?" she wondered. We were pleased by her response and encouraged her to just keep walking for thirty minutes. She walked at her own steady pace, the pace she fell into naturally. Because there was no exercise function in this session all the emphasis was on helping Barbara get more in touch with her body and on learning how she could release the tensions that built up hour by hour, day by day, in her muscles and joints.

She learned to allow her arms to extend their range of motion ever so slightly, with the movement coming from her shoulder, not her lower arm. This slight shift of awareness on her part allowed her to relax her shoulders, and the pain there dissolved. The tightness in her neck also eased when she learned to focus her eyes at a closer distance while she walked.

Barbara had a tendency to focus at an extreme distance and tilt her head slightly backward while she walked. It was almost like she didn't want to see what was in front of her but was always trying to look into the future. She said that this was her tendency since so much of her work was built around anticipating the consequences of the ongoing legal maneuvers of the cases she worked on. By bringing her body into alignment, Barbara was better able to focus on her work in the present.

Over the four-week period we worked with Barbara she reported that even in times of great pressure, she would make herself take a break and just walk the corridors of the office, keeping mindful of her new walking style. She told us that several of her colleagues noticed that "something seems different about you." Some said she seemed more alert and not as tired.

In that one short month Barbara saw and felt a shift in her body language. Her body statement changed from "I'm so burdened" to "I can handle the burden and challenges." She started to feel relieved of her chronic "heaviness." She felt more energized and less foggy. She was particularly pleased that she could continue to develop and grow on her own without having to participate in a long-term training program.

At first, she was surprised at how quickly her body adapted to these changes we taught her until she realized that the changes were really only modest corrections from the bad habits she had unconsciously developed. It was the tool of videotape, however, that affected Barbara most profoundly. This visual record spurred her to become conscious of herself in a healthy manner, not self-conscious. We encouraged her, as we do everyone, to use this powerful tool of communication, a tool that can help you gain in self-knowledge and confidence. Barbara came to understand that since how we walk is virtually ignored, except in times of recovery from injury, the very idea that adjusting a person's walking pattern could prove so beneficial seemed both radical and simple.

Useful Modern Tools

When we work with individuals on a treadmill in our office, we use the same video techniques that we are sharing with you. Probably the most difficult aspect of the video technique is viewing the tape. We have never known anyone who expressed pleasure or delight in themselves when they first see the tape. Sometimes their uneasiness and judgments come out as harsh negative assessments, sometimes in the form of nervous laughter, sometimes as grim silence. There is often a negative attitude toward oneself. Those first few frames of watching the video are usually an exercise in heavy self-criticism.

Many times, clients try to avoid the experience of taping; but for us it is a vital and necessary tool that helps people finally accept themselves, even if the viewing experience is painful or annoying or disturbing at first. Other clients are excited to see themselves and then become unhappy when they actually do view themselves. Viewing yourself walking on videotape for the first time is bound to be an emotional moment (and perhaps you will be that rare individual who is pleased with himself or herself but would still like to enhance his or her walking style). We urge you to try it, to risk all those uncomfortable feelings and then come to a point of acceptance so that you can change what can be changed peacefully, not because you "can't stand" the way you look or "hate" what your body language communicates.

The essence of life is movement and change. We have found that many people develop genuine self-esteem when they can first accept who they are and what they are, particularly in terms of their bodies . . . and that positive physical and psychological change can occur from learning balanced and centered walking.

CHAPTER 11

Walking Tools and Paraphernalia

It has to be stated that nothing special in terms of equipment is needed for walking. A good *shoe* is one of the only items that need some attention paid to. But if you look around, there are enough toys and gadgets to keep any walker satisfied and busy for years to come.

A partial listing can read as follows:

Pedometers—to keep track of how far you walk at any given time

Stopwatches—to tell you how fast you walked

Heart monitors—to tell you how hard your heart is working

Diaries—to record all your accomplishments

Sun visors—to keep the sun out while you walk

Sunscreens—to keep your skin moist and healthy

Headbands—to keep the sweat from your eyes

Sunglasses—to keep the glare from your eyes

Caps—to keep your head cool and collected

Insect repellent—to keep the bugs away

Special whistles—to keep the dogs away
Walking sticks—for support and style and security
Fanny packs—to keep all the equipment handy
Walking socks—to keep your feet in good shape
Walking underwear—for more comfort
Walking gloves—for warm hands
Walking outfits—to keep the elements tame
Walking boots—to conquer all terrains
Walking-shoe inserts—to create comfort
Walking clubs—for group support
Walking watches—to keep time and cadence
Walking music tapes—to keep you in rhythm
Walking books—to keep you informed and educated
Walking magazines—to keep you updated
Walking water bottles—to keep the thirst away
Walking compasses—to keep you in the right direction
Walking videos—for indoor walking
Walking videos—for outdoor walking
Walking professionals—to keep you on the mend and walking
Walking experts—to keep you walking in the latest trends

If we left any out, it was because we wanted go on and tell you about the perfect walking shoe.

The Perfect Walking Shoe—for You

The perfect shoe can help your body move with an easy, flowing rhythm. It can allow you to "feel" the ground below your feet. It can let you feel the earth support you against that pull of gravity. The experts in walking agree on certain principles that are important in a walking shoe.

1. A cushioned reinforced heel counter (the back of the shoe where the heel strikes first). This guides the foot through its roll forward to the toe and it prevents the foot from twisting inward (pronation) or outward (supination). This should be firm, and not overly padded to prevent instability when the foot comes down.

2. Room in the forefoot area of the shoe to allow the toes to spread out comfortably as you pushoff.

3. A lightweight shoe that is breathable. In an article in *Prevention Magazine* on shoes, Gale Malesky writes about the different schools of thought when it comes to the biomechanics of walking and the designs of "new" walking shoes. There are the "rockers" and the "flexers" schools of shoe advocates. The rockers promote a shoe that has a fairly thick, stiff sole. It has a beveled heel and toe in the sole. Its proponents suggest that the rocker profile allows the foot to be supported as the weight is transferred from heel to toe like the curve of a rocking chair. The other school believes that the sole of the walking shoe should be even more flexible than that of the running shoe. This feature allows the shoe to bend more in the forefoot region. This shoe has a thinner, much more flexible sole, allowing the shoe to bend at about forty-five degrees when pushoff occurs.

So when you go into a "walking-shoe" department and see some really thick cushioned shoes and then see walking shoes with thinner more flexible soles, therein lies some of the reason.

Of course there are other categories of shoes, such as the heavy-duty shoes based on traditional hiking-boot design. These have thick resilient insoles and outer soles but are still relatively lightweight. They are good for rugged terrain and all-day use. If you are going hiking and in rugged terrain, then definitely consider the hiking shoe. It will give you protection and support for that type of terrain. Some people prefer a flexible walking shoe for rugged terrain. To each his own.

The thick "rocker" shoe is a work horse for many walkers, but it might be creating too much of an artificial rocker for the foot. The inherent lack of flexibility of any thick shoe, especially in the forefoot area, is a restriction of a fundamental aspect of human foot motion: the push-off through the ball of the feet and toes. Much of the power that is generated in walking comes from that push-off. This limitation of a fundamental human movement can create problems in the long walk. Our premise is that the flexibility of the body, freedom of the body, good and proper use of the body are paramount.

So are we advocating bare feet?

Well, that's what our feet are primarily designed for, but we realize that down through the ages the naked foot has had trouble being accepted as a practical or comfortable all-terrain vehicle. We opt for the thinner, more flexible shoe for the level non-rugged terrain. It is lower to the ground, there is ease in the push-off, and it seems much closer to how we would walk in nature.

Historically shoe construction has reflected the saga of fashion, cultural influences, status—all this leading to a myriad of foot disorders. So shop around, try different styles and different types. Your feet will speak to you and tell you how they feel. Listen to them, they speak much truth to you.

Some Hints Whispered by Your Shoe

1. Try me out later in the day when your feet are slightly swollen.

2. If I feel snug to you don't buy me. I will not expand—contrary to what you think.

3. After you put on both of us, walk around the store and really try to feel if we are comfortable.

4. Am I flexible, do I support your weight?

5. Do I have enough space in the toe box area for you to wiggle your toes? When you push off, your toes are going to want to expand and spread. Do I have that kind of room to accommodate you? You might want to buy me a half-size larger than your normal size.

6. Is my heel firm enough? Do you sink too much and lose your stability when you plant down my heel? My heel should be firm but not too rigid.

Selecting walking shoes is no place for the "no pain, no gain" philosophy. The pure sensual comfort of your feet is your primary goal. Remember that, and you will always walk well.

Do You Want Musical Accompaniment?

Before we write another word about the portable radios and tape recorders we should mention the latest warnings about the dangers of loud music damaging your ears, not paying attention to traffic and your surroundings, playing the radio at low volume, and the increased likelihood of being mugged because you are wearing a beautiful radio. These are all valid reasons to be careful and cautious and attentive and we fully endorse the warnings. But, having mentioned the warnings, we must also say that music can do wonders for your style, your sense of rhythm, and can add much spice and life to your walk.

This modern wonder, which allows you to transport the music that was once relegated to the concert hall or your living room and have it travel with you every step of the way out to the park, road, or track, is truly a delight. But more than that, music activates a deep core rhythm in the body. We have used Afro-Brazilian music in our video-treadmill sessions at The Walking Center and have seen remarkable transformations of a walker's awkward, inhibited movements into a rhythmic, graceful flow.

The effects of music are extraordinary and should be used if you find yourself unable to get moving, when you seem to be tired and morose, when you just want to say, "I don't want to walk today." Music can get you out of your head and into your body quicker than most things you can find. It is a superb tool for dropping your inhibitions about moving your body. Music taps that ancient primitive part of you that longs to be awakened and freed. Music can make those long walks seem like minutes.

Walking With Weights

When walking was rediscovered, the benefits were still suspect. Was it really aerobic? Was it for the injured, or, worse, for wimps? So walking began to be adorned with toys and gadgets; it seemed to need something to make it acceptable. Something to qualify it for the "no pain, no gain" requirement. So people started walking with weights attached to their bodies. Some of the trendy walkers weren't just walking anymore, they were "pumping iron walking."

In order to make walking a more macho and glamorous activity, walkers have been told to carry weights ranging from 2 pounds to 120 pounds. These heavy slugs of metal are supposed to be worn around the walker's neck in the guise of a bandolero, weighted belts around the midsection, very heavy ankle weights, heavy shoes, and even heavier hands. Some gadgets are potentially harmful. Weights belong in this category.

Our experience and research about the effectiveness and correct use of weights show that two main themes stood out among the benefits. First, the added weights tend to increase your workload. You work harder to accomplish the task with the weights. Second, you increase the calorie output with added weights—but not by a very significant amount. Some studies spoke about the results of increasing muscle strength and endurance. What almost none of these studies addressed were the drawbacks and harmful physiological and biomechanical effects of using these weights improperly, or even properly as the case may be. These include:

> Distortion in posture and body alignment.
> Joint and ligament injuries, especially with ankle weights.
> Strain on shoulders and wrists.

Posture and alignment problems occur when the weights throw off the body's equilibrium and alignment, and walkers tilt their bodies awkwardly in an attempt to compensate. At best, tension in the hands and chest limits the range of motion in the swing action and detracts from the naturally fluid gait. Muscles get tired quickly and the walker stops swinging weights and just holds them almost stationary at the body's side. This sets up contraction and tension in the arms and shoulders and chest, and that tension is spread throughout the body. The weights hinder the sense of rhythm that the walker is trying to achieve and a forced mechanical gait takes over.

Furthermore, if you are on a long walk and get tired, there is no where to put down the weights. You are forced to carry them all the way home. Many walkers do not have the strength to hold hand weights in proper alignment with the rest of the arm. The weights bend the hand down setting up a chain reaction where the

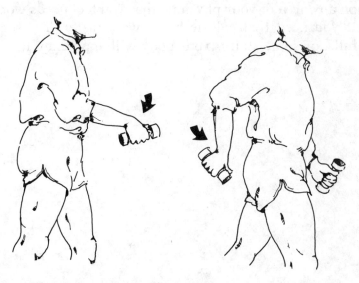

Most walkers carry weights incorrectly:
Weights carried improperly cause the wrists to bend out of alignment, leading to distortions in the arms and shoulders. (If you must use them, the weights should be light and carried in a straight-line symmetrical to the arms and wrists, with the arms swinging and not just held beside the body.)

shoulders bunch up to take over the task of carrying them.

We do not recommend the use of weights, but if you must use them, use *very* light weights, about six to eight ounces, in the form of weighted gloves to offset any gripping with the hands. We have found that the costs in wear and tear on the body and walking style far exceed any derived benefits for the majority of walkers whom we see and work with. In the hands of the athlete who is properly conditioned and trained, weights may be appropriate. Greater benefits can come from supplementing your walking with a separate program of weight training to work on upper-body strength, or on any area of your physique that you feel needs work. If you need that calorie burn, walk faster. Try some hills, or some stairs. Your body will appreciate it.

CHAPTER 12

Walking Tall— Releasing the Power Within You

Body language expresses feelings and emotions. Mable Elsworth Todd, in her book *The Thinking Body*, makes that same statement with further eloquence. She states that ". . . Often the body speaks clearly that which the tongue refuses to utter." Experts say it's possible to change those outward messages by changing the movement patterns of the body. Is it also possible to send messages inward by changing postural patterns and attitudes? Can you uplift your inner feelings by walking in a more uplifting, confident, aware manner?

The answer is a resounding YES! In fact, the psychological changes that come from consistent positive walking will probably have as much, if not more, impact on your life than the physical benefits. Since you are spending some portion of your day walking, whether that walking is a structured "fitness activity" or not, you can apply the principles of positive walking, and the benefits will accumulate over time.

You can walk well at any speed, look marvelous doing it, and get more out of it at every level: physical, emotional, and spiritual because you will be using your body in the most wholesome way possible for you. You'll look wonderful doing it—and you'll feel so wonderful doing it, you'll start doing it every time you walk. Your entire body language will start communicating your growing sense of well-being even when you are feeling blue. As you develop a healthier awareness of your body through walking well, that heightened awareness can lead to greater confidence and an increase in self-esteem.

Marjorie at fifty-two had been caught, quite unexpectedly, in the rapidly shifting life-styles of the '70s and the '80s. She was divorced at fifty; moved from the city to the suburbs, where she had to learn to drive; entered the job market at mid-life, having been a homemaker for thirty years. Now, after this turbulent shift, she was afflicted with a painful bout of depression. The move out of the city to be closer to her children had seemed bright and appealing, as well as being an economic necessity. But Marjorie felt isolated and cut off from her customary life. And while she thought of herself as strong and adaptable, the weight of these enormous changes began to eat at her confidence and composure.

When we met Marjorie at a local walking seminar she truly looked as if the weight of world were on her shoulders. She was halting and tentative when she approached us, and we could see the deep sadness in her eyes and her body. Her whole being communicated a heaviness and sorrow. "I just realized that I don't walk anymore." She was speaking to us in a hesitant manner. We could sense from this attractive, stylish woman that there was something deeply troubling her.

As they began to walk, Deena noticed that Marjorie walked with her head down and that she avoided eye contact. There was a downward pull to her body as Marjorie slowly moved forward. "Since I moved from the city I realized that I don't walk the way I used to. Before I moved here I would walk everywhere. It was just part of my life-style. I used to walk in my neighborhood to shop, to browse, to visit friends. It was part of my way of life," she said, again her voice was almost without energy, like her body.

Deena suggested to Marjorie that she lift her head a bit higher and look ahead as we walked. "I don't have anything to lift my head for anymore," she protested. "I never even thought about walking. I just did it every day. It's like I have to make time now for something I just took for granted." Her voice was filled with annoyance and anger. Before her anger emerged, Marjorie was almost leaden and plodding. But as soon as she recognized that she had been missing walking every day, the energy of her anger lifted her body. As Deena and Marjorie walked, they increased their walking speed slightly as Marjorie's feelings picked up in intensity. "I really shouldn't be talking to you like this, I'm sorry," and as she spoke, her body slumped downward again.

"It's fine with me, let's just keep on moving," Deena assured her, making moderate suggestions as they continued: "Lift your head slightly and let your feet feel the ground under you. Imagine there's a cord at your belly button pulling you along. And try to flex your foot ever so slightly before making contact with the ground." Since Marjorie had years and years of walking behind her she was able to incorporate these hints rather easily.

Soon they were walking together in rhythm with a smooth and even cadence. The energy in Marjorie's body picked up noticeably. The strength of walking together plus the relief of getting out of herself and her problems for those few minutes literally lifted her posture and her body came alive again. "It just feels good to walk again like this," she said. "I can feel some of the tension leaving my body for the first time in months. I knew I had to get moving again, but I hate the idea of having to plan to walk, of having to make it part of my schedule. That just seems so ridiculous to me. Now that I'm part of the automobile society I actually have to make time to walk. That's nonsense. You know, I just happened to be here today to do a bit of shopping. I didn't come to hear you and your husband. I wasn't even thinking about exercise or walking or anything like it. And it suddenly hit me as I was listening to you, that I haven't walked at all in the months since I moved from the city. I'll figure out a way to get back to walking again," she affirmed. "I don't feel as depressed right now. All I've been doing since I moved out here is trying to distract myself from my hurts and sorrows. Now I can think clearly again."

We said good-bye and, as Deena handed Marjorie one of our business cards, I urged her to come by and walk with us in the park if she was ever in the city. Instead, we received a wonderful letter from Marjorie about two months later. She reported that her unexpected encounter with us at the mall had helped her get back to walking. And even though she now had to "make special time" for her walks, she was able to maintain a relaxed and open approach to simply "going for a walk." She shared that her psychological stresses and depression were lifting a bit and that she had discovered a few other walkers in her apartment complex and was beginning to make some new friends. She also added that since she had the longer history as a "walker" she was the inspiration for her neighbors.

Marjorie confessed that at times of depression it was hard to move, but since she had formed a core group of walkers she would enlist a friend for comfort and companionship. She also thanked us for the walking tips and said that her legs and hips were shaping up in ways she had thought impossible for a "middle-aged woman." And, bonus of bonuses, she said that people were beginning to notice a "sparkle" and a "glow" about her.

The assault of low energy, anxiety, loneliness, procrastination, and other pessimistic symptoms burdens great numbers of people of every age, sex, and economic level. Sometimes manageable, sometimes unmanageable, the weight of depression usually brings the body to a standstill. And it is just this immobility that deepens the already low-energy state of depression. And while we don't pretend to have the magic "cure-all" for clinical depression, we have observed again and again, that walking for even ten or fifteen minutes has the effect of "lifting" people from their shallow, "down" state back into awareness, particularly if they become more attuned to their bodies by using our approach.

The convenience of simply getting one foot in front of the other is the perfect age-old antidote to glum moods. Nothing grand, to be sure. But reliable, continuous, and ever available. Whether you are walking for exercise or not, you are still walking. Walking with vigor and attention to the small but important details of that most natural and human function can bring you positive benefits that may even outweigh the effects of aerobics. Peace of mind and a sense of wellbeing are the greatest health benefits in the world.

Happier Steps

When we learned of the work of Sara Snodgrass, a psychologist at Skidmore College in New York, we were excited. Her study on the effect of walking behavior and style on mood, done in the controlled environment of a scientific laboratory, confirmed what we were learning and practicing in "real" life. She and her colleagues had observed that walkers who took short, shuffling strides with their heads down experienced fatigue and depression while walkers who took longer (but not exaggerated) strides and used their arms in a nonexaggerated swing experienced a sense of vigor and a happier mood.

Dr. Snodgrass simply observed that the way we walk can affect our mood. "This suggests that when we feel down, we can brighten our mood by purposefully walking with vigor," states the paper she prepared for the ninety-fourth annual convention of the American Psychological Association in Washington, D.C., in August 1986.

Developing better feelings toward yourself, about your body and about who and what you project to the world, are side benefits of "positive" walking that set you on the road toward inner security. The uplifting qualities of our approach tone muscles and strengthen the entire body in such a meticulous way that your body becomes your ally and partner, not an adversary to be beaten into shape or forced to become something other than its best self. As you learn the movements later on and start to incorporate them into your walk you will feel, see, and experience the confidence that comes both from doing something constructive for yourself and from the method itself. You will naturally express confidence through your posture and your walk. Genuine self-confidence is built upon many levels of personality. Using your body harmoniously on a continual basis is just one of the areas where self-confidence can grow.

Smile With Your Body and Enjoy It

Have you ever noticed the faces of people engaged in exercise? We do it all the time, and what is astounding to us is the contortions and pain and anguish registered on their facial muscles. Most of these people were going at such slow speeds that it was highly unlikely that the exertion could produce such grimaces.

Alexander Lowen, in his book *Bioenergetics*, suggests that your face is the mask you present to the world, and can reveal a lot about your inner feelings. But Ken Dychtwald, in his brilliant book *Body/Mind*, thinks that we "also shape our faces as a result of who we pretend to be and how we pretend to be feeling."

A recent article by science writer Daniel Goleman in the *The New York Times* on July 18, 1989, "A Feel-Good

Theory: A Smile Affects Mood," cited evidence of studies that suggested that the effects of facial expressions can actually induce the mood they portray. He goes on to state "that facial expressions are not just the visible sign of an emotion, but actually contribute to the feeling itself." A smile can actually help make you happier. A frown can induce sadness and possible misery. So smile and the world smiles back at you, as the old adage goes, and science now is even verifying that old wisdom.

What are you saying with your face? If you are showing anguish and pain—maybe you are walking with too much intensity for your level of fitness. Maybe you should slow down and do it more gently. But if you are in shape and are not going too fast, are you pretending you are by tensing your face into a pretzel?

Tensing your body while walking leads to undue wear and tear on your whole system. When you contort and tense your face needlessly or unconsciously, you can damage your own natural beauty. The contortions add lines and years to your face, stress to your body, and confusion to your mind. Your facial expressions can actually induce the mood they portray. So a smiling, pleasantly calm face will serve you well on many levels: body, mind, and spirit. You will not be sending mixed messages to your brain about how you feel. To quote another old-timer, Hippocrates, "Walking is the best medicine." All this wonderful medicine, free of side effects or contraindications, starts with the first step you take.

One of the key features of our walking approach is that it brings walkers to the point where they experience feeling good in their bodies. They experience feeling good in a real way for a sustained period of time—be it a moment, several moments, or much longer. They feel it in a sustained movement pattern that is fluid, graceful, and natural to the body.

Given the opportunity, the vast majority want to feel good, yet so many folks have forgotten the good feelings experienced in moving well. So remember, it does not have to burn to be good. Feeling good in the body is what a healthy life is about, what walking for life is all about. So enjoy it and smile.

CHAPTER 13

A Lifetime Walking Skill and Style

What do you do when your resolve begins to melt, your mind begins to play coy games, and you hear that nagging negative voice eating away at your determination?

"I can't . . ."
"I'll do it tomorrow . . ."
"Maybe I look silly . . ."

How do you counter that pestering, undermining part of yourself that begins to look at walking as a chore? All the conventional hints to counter the exercise drop-out effect—setting realistic goals, recording your progress, starting slow, not overdoing it, cross-training—try to address the dilemma that 60 to 70 percent of adults who start exercising drop out within the first month.

People have devised all sorts of schemes to fight the tedium of the workout—from personal stereos to working out with a companion and chattering away the time to sessions with a personal trainer. These schemes

146

are basically derived from struggling with some inner resistance to exercise. What happens when you tell yourself, "I'm too tired to exercise?" You feel more tired and you generally feel badly about yourself, and then your body language expresses this bind of fatigue and worthlessness. You're caught in a vicious circle and the escape seems hard to find. But it may be that some of those negative statements are really disguised comments which camouflage inflated expectations you have for yourself about the value and effects of exercise in your life.

If you learn to use your mind as an ally instead of an adversary then you won't be crushed by the excessive demands for perfect physical health you may have placed on yourself. The "performance" aspect of exercise will gradually diminish and the innate human drive for pleasure will soon animate you instead of some arbitrary goal to attain a perfect physique, or to have the healthiest heart on the block.

The values of exercise and fitness have been so widely extolled these past fifteen to twenty years that not to be involved in exercise or fitness in some way seems almost rebellious or un-American. Yet, the very word "exercise" connotes a regimented program or structured physical activity that one *should* do. And woe to you if you don't exercise: back problems, poor posture, overweight, overeating, bone disease, insomnia, chronic fatigue, varicose veins, high cholesterol, frequent headaches, hypertension, heart problems, constipation, digestive problems, stiff joints, general aches and pains, poor circulation, depression, and premature aging.

Reading the above catalogue of physical disturbances could be depressing in itself. It is as if you are deliberately inviting these problems into your life if you dare not exercise. And should you develop these symptoms of physical disuse then you become the guilty party because you brought it on yourself. Serves you right, says an angry, judgmental voice. That voice is nonsense. Not everyone is born to exercise.

Born to Move

But everyone is born to move. Life and movement are synonymous. Where there is life there is movement. And where there is movement there is walking. If you cooperate in the movement that you were born to do—walking—and not turn it into an exaggerated effort, you will reap all the benefits that exercise promises: increased circulation, elimination of impurities from your system by inhaling more oxygen through natural deep breathing, strengthened muscles, increased endurance and stamina, and an enhanced physical appearance.

Movement, the simplicity of natural movement, is the ongoing fact of life. As you walk about during your day you hardly consider the fact of movement. You just do it. So we are encouraging you to expand your views of movement and exercise. We want to help you break out of that limited, routinized, three-to-four-times-a-week thirty-minute regime that is continually being advocated as the minimum requirement to hold the line against the ravages of an underused body.

As the trend toward softer, slower exercise takes hold it can help you soften your own demands and evaluate your needs in the light of reason. And in the light of reason may you find walking. Not the artifice of faddish fitness walking styles, but the beauty of balanced walking—walking that goes with you everywhere.

And if you are an exercise enthusiast, we would like to encourage you to also add some balanced walking to your life. It is our conviction and experience that far too great an emphasis has been placed on physical fitness and exercise almost to the detriment of the good derived from wholesome physical activity. We have seen many, many people fall short of their goals only to slip into guilt-inducing inactivity. And frequently the slide into inactivity occurs only because those goals had nothing to do with the individual's needs or pleasures. When exercise becomes a chore it will sooner or later fall by the wayside.

But if you begin to view walking not as exercise but as pure, simple pleasure, and if you were to step away from striving for fitness, you may begin to find that you can just go for a walk without having any more of a reason than just going for a walk. And as you incorporate the steps that you have learned in this book, you will be able to generate the inner glow that comes from simply moving with awareness and consciousness. You do *not* need to structure specific time in order to get benefits from walking. It is a myth that the only good exercise is scheduled exercise that conforms to standards of achieving aerobic efficiency. There are no limits on where or when you walk. The only limits are the ones you impose on yourself by believing that a five-minute or ten-minute or fifteen-minute walk is not good enough, so why bother. You do not have to regiment yourself or be confined by time, location, or equipment in order for your body to be a happier, more smoothly running machine. Just the simplicity of a longer walk from parking spot to destination is valuable. A walk around the block is better than no walk at all. A walk through the corridors of your office building can stretch out your legs, ease the accumulation of muscular tensions in your body, and set your body humming for the next task at hand. Don't dismiss these breaks as being inconsequential. Don't deny yourself the opportunity to use walking in your behalf because you have come to believe in the minimum thirty-minute exercise ritual.

When the voice of a "fitness expert" warns against leisure walking or strolling, that voice may be sounding a deathknell for your own desire to walk at a speed that works for you. We would rather see you stroll than sit, amble pleasurably rather than do nothing. You do not have to be a prisoner to exercise.

A Permanent Tool

This approach to walking that you are learning is there as a permanent tool for you to use anytime you want. The beauty of balanced and centered walking is that it is at your feet at all times. It generally requires no great heroic effort to walk positively throughout your daily activities.

Even your own negative, sluggish, guilty thoughts can be countered with just a few steps of balanced walking because you will be using the body itself as a positive expression, which in turn will generously feed back to your mind. You will no longer have to motivate yourself, as you feel that wonderful positive flow of energy that comes from walking well, without eccentric, complicated motions.

A lifetime skill and style:
The beauty of balanced and centered walking is at your feet at all
times.

The monthly articles that appear in magazines on exercise and fitness may seem like your own cheering section, as they encourage you to do more, or do less, or do something else to extract you from the ring of boredom. But, as valuable as they may be, they may not speak to your personal needs. And it may very well be that your real needs don't conform to the popularized fitness standards that have been established in the last twenty years. Does that mean that your health will be compromised and undermined because you can't meet those standards that have been touted as "real" needs for your body? Not at all. It may just mean that you have to find your own recipe for a wholesome lifestyle.

We want to help your walking time—whatever it is—become a time of pleasure and joy. Our interests, curiosities, and healing tendencies directed us to look at the body and how it moves when walking. We saw bodies in varying states of tension, ignorance, and unconsciousness. We were particularly disturbed by the fitness-walking methods being promoted, as walking turned from "walking" to exercise. We saw mechanistic, hard-edge technique applied to natural movement. And we saw some of the basic body stresses of tight shoulders, neck, and jaw; weak, pained backs; etc. being further driven into the bodies of millions of eager fitness walkers. We saw tight, furrowed faces instead of smiles, clenched fists where we wanted to see a gently cupped hand, wildly swinging arms where we wanted to see smooth forward movement, and tight, rigid hips instead of natural, rhythmic grace.

The most beautiful part of balanced, centered, positive walking is that it provides you with a constant tool that can help relieve you of the physical and emotional symptoms of stress. All the moves and tips will soon become second nature because they derive from your own natural walking movements—again, nothing artificial, unnecessary, or exaggerated. And "soon" doesn't mean immediately, because it does take some time for your body to get used to anything even slightly unfamiliar. Remember—every footstep is built-in "practice."

Nature is always restoring balance; you can cooperate with nature and find the balance and harmony you crave by walking naturally. Until recently, the role of exercise was only to improve the physical body. Using natural exercise to enhance physical health and inner health means respecting the needs of both the body and the mind. If you use your mind to push your body to do what comes unnaturally, you generate more stress and discomfort. But if you use your body with less stress, you will free your mind and your body so that they function together with greater harmony.

Back to Pleasure

And that brings us back to pleasure. Again, deep pleasure is not an escape from discomfort. It is a state of satisfaction and delight that continually calls to us and beckons to us from our tight and stressed shadows. Pleasure is an experience, not an idea. So we hope to help you experience your walks as pleasurable and life enhancing. By learning the simple, natural moves in our book, you will open the door to an uplifting communication between your body and your mind. You can then turn that longed-for "positive" mental attitude into a reality as you use your body wisely and well. Minute by minute, day by day, you can meet the unknown with greater balance and awareness.

Several years ago when the first walking prescriptions were issued they called for "fast" walking or "brisk" walking, or "power" walking, with the implication that this was the "right" way of walking. And if you were uninterested in speed, or you were too interested in speed, this prescription set up an emotional response in you. Maybe you felt dejected or guilty or driven. And the conflict of those emotions is the wear and tear of stress. And that stress sets up static in the communication channels between your body and your mind. When you walk well you set into motion, literally, a flowing line of positive, constructive communication between these two vital systems.

Maggie Spilner, Walking Editor of *Prevention Magazine*, said, "When I take the time to focus myself on the walking approach David has taught me, I feel an instantaneous feeling of strength and power in my body. Rather than just plodding along or trudging along, I am moving with power, grace, and purpose. It's not something I have to practice six months to achieve or sustain. Once I establish the movements correctly, the feeling of power and personal authority are felt immediately." You, too, can have those feelings of power and personal authority, peace and grace.

Do Steps and Don't Steps

Before we send you on your way, here are some good tips to remember:

Do allow your hips and arms to set the rhythm and speed.

Do extend the back leg to get a maximum toe-off and stretch.

Do walk faster by taking quicker steps and not by just lengthening your stride.

Do drink plenty of water after a workout on a hot day.

Do try and eat well by the diet of your choice.

Do start slowly and gradually lengthen your workouts.

Do use walking as your everyday means of transport if possible.

Do set realistic goals to avoid the implication of failure.

Do swim, bike, run, ski, roller-skate, or any other activity to keep yourself limber and active.

Do remember to breathe.

Do become aware of the back of your body.

Do keep your hands lightly cupped, not limp like a rag doll.

Do keep that sense of touching the ground, feeling the ground, and moving off it securely. When you plant your foot you'll feel a rolling from heel to toe that will serve to straighten your leg at the knee.

Do walk for life.

Don't force your body to go faster by accelerating your arm swing.

Don't copy just anybody's walking style, it may not flatter you.

Don't slap your heel down hard on the ground, the ground may slap you back and that hurts.

Don't eat a meal within a couple of hours of a heavy workout—digestion basically stops and that food will just sit there waiting for you to stop.

Don't smoke.

Don't walk in some bizarre style just for the sake of burning off calories.

Don't overdo it.

Don't "pump" your arms. The power of your body is in the legs and hips, not the shoulders and arms.

Don't hold your arms rigidly at a ninety-degree angle. It wastes energy and unbalances the body to hold your arms like that.

Don't flail your arms around in an effort to increase your aerobic effort. You'll simply throw your body off balance. Don't move as though your upper body and your lower body were doing separate workouts.

Don't lean forward from the waist in an effort to go faster. Going faster will come naturally with time and with the building of muscles and endurance.

Don't let your belly sag. Breathe deeply and deliberately. Most of us breathe in a lazy, shallow fashion. Breathing deeply means using the diaphragm and tummy muscles to expand and contract the belly, which has to change its shape if the deeper parts of the lungs are to be used. As you get better at walking this way, it will be easier to keep your belly strong—not in an artificially constricting way, but in a natural way.

BIBLIOGRAPHY

Donaldson, Gerald. *The Walking Book.* New York: Holt, Rinehart and Winston, 1979.

Dychtwald, Ken. *Body/Mind.* New York: Jove/HBJ, 1978.

Goleman, Daniel. "A Feel-Good Theory: A Smile Affects Mood." *The New York Times,* July 18, 1989, p. C1.

Jackson, Ian. *The Breathplay Approach to Wholelife Fitness.* Garden City, New York: Doubleday and Co., Inc., 1986.

Lowen, Alexander. *Bioenergetics.* New York: Penguin Books, 1976.

———, *Narcissism—The Denial of the True Self.* New York: Collier Books, 1985.

Maleskey, Gale. "These Shoes Are Made for Walking." *Prevention Magazine,* September 1986.

Mann, Ralph. "A Biomechanical Analysis of Sprinters." *Track Technique,* TAC/USA, Winter 1986, p. 3000-3003.

Rolf, Ida. *Rolfing: The Integration of Human Structure.* Santa Monica, California: Dennis Landman Publishers, 1977.

Todd, Mable Elsworth. *The Thinking Body.* Brooklyn, New York: Dance Horizons, 1972.

Westerfield, Gary, ed. *The Racewalking Coach.* Vol. 1, No. 1–4. Smithtown, New York, 1987–1989.

Whatever your age, life-style, and fitness level, Perigee has a walking program for you.

The oldest and yet "newest" form of exercise, walking can increase both your physical and your mental well-being.

Fitness Walking
by Robert Sweetgall with James Rippe, M.D., and Frank Katch, Ed.D. *illustrated with line drawings and 60 black-and-white photographs*

Whether you have survived a heart attack, are elderly or on a weight-loss program, or are walking "for the health of it," *Fitness Walking* has invigorating but safe programs that include beginning to advanced walking exercises. Robert Sweetgall, a dedicated fitness walker, is the only man to travel all fifty United States on foot. Both Dr. Rippe, a Harvard-trained cardiologist, and Dr. Katch are health and fitness experts at the University of Massachusetts, Dr. Rippe director of the Medical School for Health, Fitness, and Human Performance, and Dr. Katch professor and chairman of the Department of Exercise Science.

Fitness Walking for Women
by Anne Kashiwa and James Rippe, M.D.

Although walking is an ideal activity for everyone, women have special fitness goals, needs, and concerns. Anne Kashiwa, an aerobics and fitness instructor and consultant, and Dr. James Rippe, a coauthor of *Fitness Walking*, have collaborated for the perfect low-impact exercise program. Their book covers weight loss, injury management, fitness during pregnancy, aerobic conditioning, muscle toning, walking for older women, stress reduction, determining fitness level, and more.

These books are available at your local bookstore or wherever books are sold. You may also order by calling 1-800-631-8571 or sending your order to:

The Putnam Publishing Group
390 Murray Hill Parkway, Dept. B
East Rutherford, NJ 07073

		PRICE	
	SBN	U.S.	CANADA
Fitness Walking	399-51149	$8.95	$11.75
Fitness Walking for Women	399-51407	8.95	12.50

*Postage & handling: $1.00	Subtotal	$	_____
for 1 book, 25¢ for each ad-	Postage & handling*	$	_____
ditional book up to a max-	Sales Tax	$	_____
imum of $3.50	(CA, NJ, NY, PA)		
	Total Amount Due	$	_____
	Payable in U.S. Funds		
	(No cash orders accepted)		

Please send me the titles I've checked above.
Enclosed is my ☐ check ☐ money order
Please charge my ☐ Visa ☐ MasterCard
Card # _____ Expiration date _____
Signature as on charge card _____
Name _____
Address _____
City _____ State _____ Zip _____
Please allow six weeks for delivery. Prices subject to change without notice.